THE Hungry Girl DIET

Also by Lisa Lillien

Hungry Girl:
Recipes and Survival Strategies for Guilt-Free Eating in the Real World

Hungry Girl 200 Under 200:
200 Recipes Under 200 Calories

Hungry Girl 1-2-3:
The Easiest, Most Delicious, Guilt-Free Recipes on the Planet

Hungry Girl Happy Hour:
75 Recipes for Amazingly Fantastic Guilt-Free Cocktails & Party Foods

Hungry Girl 300 Under 300:
300 Breakfast, Lunch & Dinner Dishes Under 300 Calories

Hungry Girl Supermarket Survival:
Aisle by Aisle, HG-Style!

HUNGRY GIRL TO THE MAX!
The Ultimate Guilt-Free Cookbook

Hungry Girl 200 Under 200 Just Desserts:
200 Recipes Under 200 Calories

Hungry Girl: The Official Survival Guides:
Tips & Tricks for Guilt-Free Eating
(audio book)

Hungry Girl Chew the Right Thing:
Supreme Makeovers for 50 Foods You Crave
(recipe cards)

THE Hungry Girl DIET

BIG PORTIONS. BIG RESULTS.
DROP 10 POUNDS
IN 4 WEEKS

Lisa Lillien

St. Martin's Griffin
New York

This book is not intended as a substitute for the medical advice of physicians. Before embarking on this or any weight-loss plan, consult a health-care professional. A number of factors influence individual weight loss. Results on the plan may vary.

The author's references to various brand-name products and services are for informational purposes only and are not intended to suggest endorsement or sponsorship of the author or her book by any company, organization, or owner of any brand.

THE HUNGRY GIRL DIET. Copyright © 2014 by Hungry Girl, Inc. All rights reserved. Printed in the United States of America. For information, address St. Martin's Press, 175 Fifth Avenue, New York, N.Y. 10010.

www.stmartins.com

Cover design and book design by Elizabeth Hodson
Food styling and photography by
        Photographer: Heather Winters
        Food Stylists: Denise Vivaldo, Cindie Flannigan

Library of Congress Cataloging-in-Publication Data

Lillien, Lisa.
  The hungry girl diet / Lisa Lillien. -- First edition.
     pages cm
  ISBN 978-0-312-67679-7 (hardcover)
  ISBN 978-1-4668-4205-2 (e-book)
  1. Reducing diets--Recipes. 2. Women--Health and hygiene. I. Title.
  RM222.2.L4777 2014
  613.2'5--dc23
                         2013045883

St. Martin's Griffin books may be purchased for educational, business, or promotional use. For information on bulk purchases, please contact Macmillan Corporate and Premium Sales Department at 1-800-221-7945, extension 5442, or write specialmarkets@macmillan.com.

First Edition: April 2014

10 9 8 7 6 5 4 3 2 1

This book is dedicated to the memory of
Matthew Shear, who was not only a huge
supporter and driving force in the success of
all of my books, but also a brilliant and
wonderful man whose smile and hearty
laugh lit up every room he entered.

Want More Hungry Girl?

Sign up for free daily emails at hungry-girl.com.

Join the Hungry Girl conversation on Facebook at facebook.com/hungrygirl.

Follow @hungrygirl on Twitter.

Check out Hungry Girl on Pinterest at pinterest.com/hungrygirl.

Follow Lisa on Instagram under the name hungrygirl.

Catch the TV show *Hungry Girl* on Food Network and Cooking Channel.

CONTENTS

SNACKS
Savvy Snackin'!

ACKNOWLEDGMENTS

First and foremost, a thank-you to my partner in crime and left-hand human, Jamie Goldberg, whose never-ending passion and dedication to Hungry Girl are appreciated more than words could ever say.

A million thank-yous to the following fabulous members of the Hungry Girl team, whose hard work helped make this book a reality . . .

Lynn Bettencourt
Michelle Ferrand
Amanda Pisani
Elizabeth Hodson

Dana DeRuyck
Callie Pegadiotes
Elaine Low

I'd also like to thank the rest of the dedicated HG staff for their support and general awesomeness . . .

Alison Kreuch
Marie Tancin
Julie Leonard

Lisa Daniels
Sandi Bourbeau

More thank-yous go out to the following amazing people . . .

Neeti Madan
John Murphy
Anne Marie Tallberg
Bill Stankey
Jeff Becker
Denise Vivaldo
David Holifield
Jackie Mgido
Sara Mallen

Jennifer Enderlin
John Karle
John Vaccaro
Tom Fineman
Heather Winters
Cindie Flannigan
Jack Pullan
Katie Killeavy

Lots of love and appreciation to my fantastic parents, sensational siblings, and incredible husband . . .

Florence and Maurice Lillien
Jay Lillien

Meri Lillien
Daniel Schneider

And a very special thank-you to the one-in-a-million David Grotto, MS, RDN, LDN, for his contributions to this book, support, expertise, advice, and friendship.

THE Hungry Girl DIET

INTRODUCTION

Hi! I'm Lisa Lillien, a.k.a. Hungry Girl.

Since 2004, I've been sending people daily emails that give advice and recommendations about guilt-free eating: enjoying foods that are delicious and satisfying, yet diet friendly. This information typically comes in the form of product finds, recipes, and tips 'n tricks—all very helpful tools when it comes to weight management. In fact, I've met tens of thousands of Hungry Girl fans over the years who have lost significant amounts of weight and credit Hungry Girl emails and cookbooks as key components of their success.

But since the beginning, people have been asking for a direct method to help them lose weight—a cohesive plan that combines everything they know and love about Hungry Girl. I've finally decided the time is right to fulfill that need and give HG fans (and the rest of the world) something they've been craving for a very long time—a simple, satisfying, and FAST weight-loss solution: THE HUNGRY GIRL DIET. It's an easy-to-follow jump-start plan that you can use to do any of the following:

1. Kick off a brand-new weight-loss journey in a major way

2. Quickly drop 5 to 15 pounds

3. Overcome a plateau in weight loss or reinvigorate a current diet plan

4. Start a new lifestyle with fresh ideas that can be used indefinitely

There's no real secret to losing weight. It's all about consuming fewer calories than you burn. But the calories that you take in have to be nutritious and satisfying. And the method of calorie control has to be something you can live with and feel good about. Otherwise, you'll never stick with it. Some diets require you to eat only small portions; others permit you to eat larger servings but limit you to foods that are bland or boring; and some diets are simply too restrictive or just plain weird! Plans like these are not only hard to follow—they're nearly impossible to maintain. It's no wonder most diets fail.

With this in mind, the basic philosophy of The Hungry Girl Diet was born: Enjoy the foods you love in nutritious ways that leave you feeling satisfied and satiated. Eat more, weigh less. Most diets try to restrict you to small and unfulfilling portions, but the bottom line is this: We all want to eat a lot of food! We're hungry, and no one wants to feel hungry when they're trying to lose weight. Over the years, I have literally made it my job and my number-one focus to find and develop guilt-free food options that satisfy cravings and give you the most bang for your calorie buck—delicious foods you can eat a lot of without taking in too many calories and grams of fat. In addition to these indispensable food finds and creations, this plan includes countless tips and tricks that I've uncovered along the way.

The Hungry Girl Diet utilizes a decade's worth of trusted food findings and philosophies that make it easy, enjoyable, and even FUN (truly!) to cut calories and lose weight. It brings them together for the FIRST TIME EVER in a comprehensive and balanced weight-loss program. The magic of The Hungry Girl Diet is that you can indulge in BIG portions of the foods you crave: fettuccine Alfredo, tacos, lo mein, chicken Parmesan, and so much more. And when you're following a food plan that allows you to eat such large, delicious, and filling meals and snacks, it's almost impossible to fail.

The four-week plan emphasizes higher consumption of protein, fruits, and vegetables; lower starchy carb intake; and moderate consumption of healthy fats. It features highly satisfying and impressively large portions. Each day consists of three meals and three snacks (I told you that you won't be hungry!), totaling about 1,300 calories. There's also a 1,500-calorie option for those who are more than 75 pounds overweight, are vigorous exercisers, or feel that a 1,300-calorie target is too aggressive for them.

No two people are exactly alike when it comes to diets and how they react to food. What works for one person might not work for someone else. That's why this isn't exactly a cookie-cutter food plan. This program will help determine what types of foods are most satisfying to you. You might learn that eating particular foods at certain times of the day makes you hungrier . . . or less hungry. The plan will guide you through these discoveries. And the findings will enable you to choose meals and snacks that work for YOUR personal needs for weight loss and weight management. Amazingly simple but incredibly helpful! And you'd be surprised to know that most people (and many other diets) never even consider the value of a personalized approach.

This diet is laid out as a four-week plan, but you can follow it for as long as you want. It has been thoughtfully devised and not only includes meal and snack choices that are satisfying and effective for weight loss, but also provides ideas and concepts you'll LOVE and can live with forever. The Hungry Girl Diet allows you to choose foods that can help you to lose weight *and* maintain your weight loss. And it's invaluable as a complement to other diet plans; you can use it in conjunction with any value-based diet plan that allows you to be flexible with your food choices. (This is key!)

If you think diets mean deprivation, I don't blame you: A lot of what's out there IS unrealistically restrictive and practically impossible to stick to. That's precisely why I developed this plan—to show you that it's 100 percent possible to eat the foods you crave, to enjoy large and satisfying portions, and to find a customizable approach that works for you. All while watching numbers on the scale go down, inches fall off your body, and clothing sizes drop. Try it and see . . .

HUNGRY GIRL'S TOP ATE REASONS THIS DIET WILL WORK FOR YOU . . .

1. BIG PORTIONS. You won't be hungry on this plan. I'm sure of it. You get three hugely satisfying meals each day, plus three impressive snacks. From large breakfast burritos to ginormous bowls of pasta, this is truly like no diet you've ever tried!

2. FLEXIBILITY. This plan provides the ideal balance of structure and freedom. With so many perfectly balanced options, you can design the exact meal plan that works for you. Mix 'n match!

3. ZERO DEPRIVATION. Whether you're craving pizza, chocolate, pasta, French fries, or even a margarita, you CAN have it . . . all while losing weight on this plan! And with HG's super-sizing and swapping techniques, you'll get satisfying portions that are completely guilt-free.

4. EASY TO FOLLOW. No complicated recipes or crazy restrictions here. The meals and snacks are incredibly simple to prepare, with many grab-n-go options as well. And this book provides you with everything you need to make diet-friendly choices when dining out.

5. SECRETS FOR SUCCESS. The pages of this book are crammed with tips and tricks that make weight loss almost effortless. You'll learn how to plan ahead, make great choices, and establish healthy habits you'll have for life.

6. TRIED-AND-TRUE CONCEPTS. Hungry Girl has been a major force in the weight-management arena for 10 years now. And with more than 2 million fans reading HG's free daily emails and content, my team and I are constantly receiving feedback and using it to perfect the meals, snacks, and strategies that people want and need. This plan employs the best of the best.

7. DIETER TESTED, REGISTERED DIETITIAN APPROVED.
In four weeks on the plan, a diverse group of testers lost an average of 10 pounds, and many dropped between 10 and 20! And since I'm not a nutritionist (I'm just hungry!), I made sure the diet received the seal of approval from a renowned registered dietitian.

8. NO GUESSWORK. Some plans leave it to you to decipher the right portions and ingredients, creating too much room for inevitable human error. The Hungry Girl Diet plan is foolproof, giving you ALL the tools you need to make the number on the scale zoom down!

FAQs

How can you have a diet plan if you are not a registered dietitian or medical professional?

I've been creating Hungry Girl content for 10 years now. And in that time, I've honed my "mad scientist" skills in the kitchen, becoming an expert at putting together meals and snacks that are delicious, incredibly satisfying, and completely guilt-free. But, I'm *not* a dietitian or medical professional. This is why the plan is 100 percent approved by an esteemed registered dietitian, David Grotto, MS, RDN, LDN.

When the idea for a Hungry Girl diet book began swirling in my brain, the very first call I made was to Dave, who is a Hungry Girl supporter and one of the most knowledgeable and approachable nutrition experts I've ever encountered. Dave has been involved with the development of this plan every step of the way, and he's been kind enough to offer up his own tips that you can incorporate while following the Hungry Girl plan.

Do I have to cook daily and follow complicated recipes on this plan?

No. Although this book does feature 60 or so recipes, many of them are extremely simple and more like food assembly than actual cooking. The meal options that do involve cooking are pretty basic and don't take long to whip up. This book also provides tons of shortcuts and alternatives. So if you love spending time in the kitchen, great, go for it! But you can absolutely follow this plan while barely lifting a skillet. The great thing about the HG diet is that there are so many choices.

Can I dine out while following The Hungry Girl Diet?

Yes. This book provides you with specific advice and the best options when having breakfast, lunch, or dinner while out and about. You should, however, prepare your own meals as often as possible during the four-week plan. This offers you the most control. When you dine out, what winds up on your plate is dependent on other people. Sure, you can special order and eyeball portions, but you'll never know if your food was prepared exactly as advertised or if the serving sizes are spot-on. Extra oil and other hidden ingredients can easily find their way into your meal, dramatically changing the calorie count. So, while dining out is okay, you'll get the best weight-loss results if you keep those restaurant trips to a minimum for the four weeks you are on the plan.

How much can I expect to lose?

There are a number of factors that influence individual weight loss: starting weight, activity level, personal metabolism, and more. That said, before this book went to print, a diverse sample of people throughout the country participated in a trial of The Hungry Girl Diet plan. The average weight loss over four weeks was 10 pounds, and many plan testers lost between 10 and 20!

Does this plan include a lot of packaged foods, or is it mostly made up of natural foods?

As you may already know, the Hungry Girl daily emails feature both packaged foods (some of which are processed) and natural foods in an effort to provide readers with information on the wide variety of foods available on store shelves. The Hungry Girl Diet, however, mainly focuses on natural foods: lean protein (poultry, fish, etc.), fat-free and reduced-fat dairy, fruits, vegetables, and more. There are a few staples that are packaged, but even many of those are all-natural. The diet employs Hungry Girl techniques, like super-sizing portions with smart ingredients, and the result is a plan filled with foods that are nutritious and satisfying.

Can vegetarians follow this diet?

Yes. While it wasn't specifically designed for vegetarians, it is possible to follow this four-week jump-start plan without eating any meat. See the Vegetarian Meals and Meatless Alternatives section on page 118 for more on this subject. It is not possible, however, for vegans to follow this plan, because the diet prominently features foods like egg whites and fat-free Greek yogurt. And although there are vegan alternatives for these foods out there, the nutritional profiles don't always line up with the dairy staples in the diet.

Can I incorporate recipes from the Hungry Girl daily emails and cookbooks into the diet?

The recipes included here were specially developed for the four-week jump-start plan. They contain key ratios of nutrients like carbs, protein, and fiber. Other HG recipes won't necessarily work on the plan, so stick with the meals and snacks in this book. You can (and should!), however, incorporate recipes from the Hungry Girl emails and cookbooks into your continued weight loss and maintenance *after* the four-week plan. See page 222 for more info.

Can I follow The Hungry Girl Diet plan while on another weight-loss program or diet?

Yes, definitely! While the plan is not affiliated with (or endorsed by) any other programs or diets, The Hungry Girl Diet plan provides many options, so you can choose foods that help you stay at or below a specified daily target set by another flexible program or diet.

DAVE'S RAVES . . .
TIPS FROM THE REGISTERED DIETITIAN!

Here's some valuable advice from David Grotto, MS, RDN, LDN . . .

Get Supplement Savvy

It can be difficult to meet all your nutrient needs through diet alone. Besides, not everyone (including this dietitian!) eats perfectly all the time. That's why I recommend taking a multivitamin supplement. Find one that's both gender and age specific, since it will be tailored to your needs.

Omega fats are important for brain and heart health. I strongly recommend taking an omega-3 fish oil supplement while on this program. (Unless you choose to have salmon two to three times per week during the later stages of the plan.) Look for one that provides 1 gram of omega-3 fats per day.

You may want to talk to a registered dietitian or your doctor for specific dietary-supplement recommendations for your individual health needs.

Water 101

The Hungry Girl Diet is high in fiber and fluids, both very good things. However, if you don't drink plenty of water, your digestive system may be thrown off a bit by the increased fiber. So drink up, and drink often!

Speaking of which, the popular "eight 8-ounce glasses a day" recommendation included in The Hungry Girl Diet plan is a good ballpark figure. Individual needs do vary, though, depending on factors like physical activity and the weather. Pay attention to body cues, and adjust your intake as needed.

Medication Management

If you are on medications to control blood pressure, cholesterol, blood sugar, or any other condition, check with your physician before embarking on this (or any) diet plan. As you lose weight, medications may need to be adjusted or discontinued, depending on your individual response to changes in diet.

Change, Change, Change . . .

New dietary and lifestyle habits are often accompanied by changes in your digestive system (read: bathroom breaks). This is perfectly normal. However, if you ever have concerns, check in with a qualified health professional.

David Grotto, MS, RDN, LDN, is the author of *101 Optimal Life Foods, 101 Foods That Could Save Your Life*, and *The Best Things You Can Eat*. He is the president and founder of Nutrition Housecall, LLC; a blogger for Real Life Nutrition WebMD; a nutrition adviser for *Fitness* magazine; and a member of both the advisory board of the Chicago Food and Nutrition Network and the advisory board of the Benedictine University Nutrition Department. In addition to all these things, he is also a trusted friend and colleague.

BEFORE YOU START . . .

Consult a doctor before embarking on any weight-loss plan. There's a reason everyone says this—it's important!

Weigh in. It's extremely beneficial to know your starting weight so you can monitor your progress. This will help you to recognize successes and spot missteps. No matter what the scale says, don't get bummed out by the number. It's just information, and that number WILL drop if you follow the plan. When you weigh in throughout the plan, do it at the same time of day and in the same type of clothing (or in NO clothes, if you like seeing lower numbers!) so that those variables don't influence the results.

Get a food scale. It doesn't need to be fancy or digital, and it doesn't need to talk to you or recognize foods when you wave them in front of it. All it needs to do is accurately weigh the items you intend to eat. It's that simple. Measuring cups and spoons are also must-haves.

Prepare to keep a food journal. As cliché as this sounds, writing down what you eat is unbelievably helpful for weight loss. It holds you accountable and also reminds you of what you've eaten. It's easy to overlook the things we pop into our mouths throughout the day—a handful of nuts here, a few M&Ms there . . . The calories DO add up. So write down what you eat. Everything.

Plan ahead, and hit the supermarket. Rather than
telling you EXACTLY what to eat, the HG plan offers lots of nutritionally
balanced options that can be mixed and matched. This way, you can
choose what works for you. So before you head out to the grocery
store, look ahead and decide what meals and snacks you want to have
for the days ahead. The supermarket list (page 90) is filled with staple
foods to get you started!

For more tools
for success—including
an app that lets you create
custom shopping lists and
track your food—visit
hungry-girl.com/diet!

DIET TIPS 'N TRICKS CHEAT SHEET!

A lot of helpful information is sprinkled throughout the diet plan section of the book. Feel free to skip ahead and read it all at once! Then revisit your favorite tips throughout the plan as needed. Here's a handy guide for easy reference . . .

Essential Reading

Secrets of Successful HG Dieters

Quick and Thrifty Tips 'n Tricks

Craving Control

Snack Attack

Dining Out

DIET TIPS 'N TRICKS CHEAT SHEET! (CONTINUED)

All Things Beverages

Beat Defeat

Mix Things Up

Plus . . .

HUNGRY GIRL DIET RESOURCES

Supermarket List of Diet-Plan Staples

Dining Out on the Plan

The Sodium Situation

Helpful How-Tos

HG's High-Fiber Veggies

HG's High-Volume Veggies

Hungry Girl's Guide to Exercise

Vegetarian Meals and Meatless Alternatives

WEEK 1

Welcome to The Hungry Girl Diet plan!

In Week 1, you'll be introduced to some staple Hungry Girl meals. These classics can (and should!) be enjoyed throughout the entire four-week plan. Try them all to see what works best for you. You might be surprised to discover a new favorite!

Here's a little guide to the Week 1 meals. You can find the full "recipes" starting on page 122 (all single servings, of course!) . . . but honestly, they're more like quick how-tos than full-on recipes. SO EASY!

Mega Fruit 'n Yogurt Bowl: This is as delicious and satisfying as it is simple. Customize it with your favorite fruit (I'm obsessed with having Fuji apples in mine) and choice of nuts (almonds are my preference). I'm a huge fan of all kinds of yogurt, but the reason I've chosen 0% (a.k.a. fat-free) Greek yogurt as a breakfast choice for this plan is because it's packed with protein—and it's thick and creamy. Even if you think you might not like it, I encourage you to try it. The optional sweetener makes it less tart. This is a great option for busy mornings.

Egg Scramble & Bun: "Egg mugs" are some of the most popular Hungry Girl creations in existence: They're egg scrambles that are made in the microwave. Egg mugs are very easy to make and require hardly any cleanup. If you prefer, you can make these in a skillet. A side of berries and a bun with light butter make this a satisfying meal.

Growing Oatmeal B-fast: I love oatmeal, but I've always found that a traditional serving is tiny and not satisfying. So the Hungry Girl "growing oatmeal" concept was born. By doubling the amount of liquid and the cook time, you get a HUGE portion of oatmeal for the same number of calories. Brilliant! This one takes a little time, but it's well worth it. There's even a time-saving microwave version! Pair with a side of hard-boiled (or scrambled) egg whites, or mix in some protein powder.

Ginormous Salad: Tremendous salads are fantastic. This is definitely my number-one lunch choice. And since there are so many different options (chicken, turkey, or tuna; black beans, chickpeas, or kidney beans; snap peas, bell peppers, or carrots; etc.), it's completely possible to have an entirely new salad every day of the week. You can also go the easy route with a bagged mix (totally acceptable!)—just add protein and beans.

Super-Sized Sandwich Platter: I love 100-calorie flat sandwich buns—they're great and have a lot of surface area—but light bread slices also work. Just like the salad, you can change things up daily by varying your protein, veggies, and more. Don't miss the tips for packing your sandwich platter to go!

Veggie 'n Bean Bowl with Side of Greek Yogurt:

A fantastic vegetarian option, mix 'n match style! I like it with mushrooms, zucchini, and black beans. The feta adds so much flavor, and the protein-packed yogurt makes it very filling. Pack it for lunch—it's good on the go!

HG-ified Fish or Chicken with Hot Veggies and Salad:

Seriously satisfying dinner. A few key items make this so flavorful, it's almost unbelievable. And with so many different proteins, sauces, and veggies to choose from (are you sensing a theme?), there are limitless variations. SO GOOD!

Chicken Hungry Girlfredo Bowl: If you're already pretty familiar with Hungry Girl, you probably associate Girlfredo Bowls with tofu shirataki noodles, my favorite low-carb (and low-calorie!) pasta swap. However, this meal can be made with another noodle alternative: broccoli cole slaw. Once softened, those shredded broccoli stems take on a noodle-like texture. Either way, you get a deliciously creamy and filling Alfredo bowl.

HG's Special Stir-Fry: This one's extremely easy to make and very filling. And with so many sauce selections, you can change up the flavor every time. Plus, there's a super-fast variation of this meal that practically makes itself.

All About Snacks . . .

In addition to three of those meals a day, choose any three snacks from the Snacks section (page 184). There are grab-n-go finds, speedy snacks, and recipes too. Just like with the meals, I recommend you try lots of different snacks to discover what works best for you. There are options with huge serving sizes, large protein counts, lots of fiber . . . Sometimes all three! There are also smart snacks to attack cravings for things like chocolate, potato chips . . . even pizza and French fries! So spend some time in the Snacks section, and find the stuff you love.

Water, Water, EVERYWHERE

I feel strongly that drinking water is key when trying to lose weight. It keeps you hydrated and energized, and it can even stop you from feeling hungry. With every meal and snack, have at least 8 ounces of water. It's easy to forget about water throughout the day, but by just making a point to have it with every meal and snack, you'll get in 48 ounces. Have at least two more 8-ounce glasses of water throughout the day. My personal favorite way to ensure that I drink lots of water is to keep it at room temperature. It's easier to guzzle that way! Using a straw also helps a LOT. And if you find plain water boring, you can flavor it up with lemon, lime, or even cucumber slices.

The Calorie Tally (and Supplemental Snacks)

It all adds up to about 1,300 calories per day. If you have 75 pounds or more to lose, have a vigorous exercise routine, or feel this calorie level is too aggressive for you, consider adding one of the following supplemental snacks to your day.

* 100 calories' worth of fruit (see HG's Fruit Chart on page 192) with 6 ounces fat-free plain Greek yogurt

* 100 calories' worth of fruit (see HG's Fruit Chart on page 192) with ½ ounce almonds or pistachios (about 12 almonds or 24 pistachios)

* 3 ounces (about 6 slices) no-salt-added turkey breast with 100 calories' worth of veggies (see HG's Veggie Chart on page 193)

Guess What?

You're ready to get started! There are many more tips 'n tricks and lots of helpful info throughout the pages of this week's plan. Don't be afraid to skip ahead and read them all at once!

Hot Tip! Lemon Water at Breakfast

While people have been debating whether it promotes fat burning or stimulates your metabolism, I drink hot water with lemon because I like the way it tastes, and I feel it's a cleaner way to start the day than coffee or tea (especially since I'd likely add sweetener to those). I also find that it helps fill me up. Just add a wedge of fresh lemon or a squirt from a bottle. Give it a shot for a few days, and see how you like it! (You can always have your coffee after.)

Need-to-Know Info: Beverage Basics

This advice might be obvious, but I'm not taking chances. Juice, soda, energy drinks . . . These drinks can add hundreds of calories to your day and seriously impede weight loss. Instead of fruit juice, have a piece of fruit as one of your snacks. The fruit has fiber and is much more filling. If you just want something sweet to drink, go for a zero-calorie beverage, like sugar-free iced tea or a fruit-flavored drink. I suggest having no more than two of these a day, though, since they do contain a few calories and can actually make you feel hungrier.

DAY 1

BREAKFAST

8 ounces hot, room-temp, or cold water

Choose one of the following:
* Mega Fruit 'n Yogurt Bowl (page 124)
* Egg Scramble & Bun (page 125)
* Growing Oatmeal B-fast (page 126)

LUNCH

8 ounces room-temp or cold water

Choose one of the following:
* Ginormous Salad with Chicken, Turkey, or Tuna (page 128)
* Super-Sized Sandwich Platter with Tuna, Turkey, or Chicken (page 131)
* Veggie 'n Bean Bowl with Side of Greek Yogurt (page 132)

DINNER

8 ounces room-temp or cold water

Choose one of the following:
* HG-ified Fish or Chicken with Hot Veggies and Salad (page 134)
* Chicken Hungry Girlfredo Bowl (page 136)
* HG's Special Stir-Fry (page 138)

SNACKS

Choose any THREE snacks from the following:
* Grab-n-Go Snacks (page 188)
* Speedy Snacks (page 186)
* Snack Recipes (page 187)

Have each with 8 ounces room-temp or cold water.

HG Reminder: Don't forget to have two additional 8-ounce glasses of water throughout the day!

Measure Up!

It's very important to weigh and measure your ingredients. Weight loss is largely based on calories in versus calories out. And if you're not properly weighing and measuring your food, you could be taking in more calories than you think.

Need-to-Know Info: Mega Meal Mania!

This plan includes HUGE and filling meals, super-sized with lots of vegetables. If you feel full before finishing a meal, save the rest for later in the day. It'll be there if you get hungry and keep you from turning to unplanned snacks. You can even split a meal into two mini meals. I do, however, encourage you to eat all of each day's food at some point during that day.

Food Cues: Breakfast Edition

Pay attention to how satisfied you feel after having each of the different breakfasts this week. Everyone reacts differently to food. Do you feel full for a long time after eating one breakfast but get hungry quickly after eating another? Jot down these discoveries, and then make morning meal choices based on that valuable info.

DAY 2

BREAKFAST

8 ounces hot, room-temp, or cold water

Choose one of the following:
* Mega Fruit 'n Yogurt Bowl (page 124)
* Egg Scramble & Bun (page 125)
* Growing Oatmeal B-fast (page 126)

LUNCH

8 ounces room-temp or cold water

Choose one of the following:
* Ginormous Salad with Chicken, Turkey, or Tuna (page 128)
* Super-Sized Sandwich Platter with Tuna, Turkey, or Chicken (page 131)
* Veggie 'n Bean Bowl with Side of Greek Yogurt (page 132)

DINNER

8 ounces room-temp or cold water

Choose one of the following:
* HG-ified Fish or Chicken with Hot Veggies and Salad (page 134)
* Chicken Hungry Girlfredo Bowl (page 136)
* HG's Special Stir-Fry (page 138)

SNACKS

Choose any THREE snacks from the following:
* Grab-n-Go Snacks (page 188)
* Speedy Snacks (page 186)
* Snack Recipes (page 187)

Have each with 8 ounces room-temp or cold water.

HG FYI: That Girlfredo Bowl can be made with tofu shirataki noodles OR bagged broccoli cole slaw. Try both, and see which you like more!

Quick Tricks for Dining-Out Success

While preparing your own food is the best way to guarantee weight loss on this plan, dining out is a part of life, and you're going to do it once in a while. Use this week to really memorize what common portions on the plan look like. This way, you'll be able to enjoy diet-friendly meals while you're out.

Check restaurant websites before you go. Then decide what you're going to have ahead of time. That way you'll avoid making on-the-spot selections when you're already there and hungry. So simple, and REALLY smart!

For a full-on guide to dining out on The Hungry Girl Diet plan, turn to page 98!

Need-to-Know Info: Eat *Everything* on the Plan

The diet is specially balanced to keep you fully nourished and satisfied, so everything counts: veggies, protein, fruit, healthy fats like nuts and olive oil . . . All important. Follow the meals closely, and don't leave anything out. Remember, you can always save leftovers for later in the day.

Wondering About Workouts?

Exercising—even a little bit—can really speed up your weight loss. Check out the exercise guide on page 112 for ideas and motivation!

DAY 3

BREAKFAST

8 ounces hot, room-temp, or cold water

Choose one of the following:
* Mega Fruit 'n Yogurt Bowl (page 124)
* Egg Scramble & Bun (page 125)
* Growing Oatmeal B-fast (page 126)

LUNCH

8 ounces room-temp or cold water

Choose one of the following:
* Ginormous Salad with Chicken, Turkey, or Tuna (page 128)
* Super-Sized Sandwich Platter with Tuna, Turkey, or Chicken (page 131)
* Veggie 'n Bean Bowl with Side of Greek Yogurt (page 132)

DINNER

8 ounces room-temp or cold water

Choose one of the following:
* HG-ified Fish or Chicken with Hot Veggies and Salad (page 134)
* Chicken Hungry Girlfredo Bowl (page 136)
* HG's Special Stir-Fry (page 138)

SNACKS

Choose any THREE snacks from the following:
* Grab-n-Go Snacks (page 188)
* Speedy Snacks (page 186)
* Snack Recipes (page 187)

Have each with 8 ounces room-temp or cold water.

Time-Saving Shortcuts!

If a meal calls for high-fiber vegetables . . .
Look for frozen and canned varieties—no cutting or cooking needed! Check the labels to make sure no other ingredients have been added. (Look for salt-free varieties.) If frozen, thaw overnight in the fridge or just pop them in the microwave.

Canned high-fiber veggies: tomatoes, green beans, carrots

Frozen high-fiber veggies (individual or mixed): bell peppers, onions, green beans, sugar snap peas, snow peas, bean sprouts, broccoli, Brussels sprouts, carrots

Packaged finds! Bagged broccoli cole slaw, which is mainly shredded broccoli stems and carrots. You can also often find fresh stir-fry mixes of onions and bell peppers.

If a meal calls for high-volume veggies . . .
You can go with frozen or canned versions here as well. Again, check the ingredients to make sure nothing's been added. (No-salt options are best.) Thaw or nuke the frozen veggies, and they'll be ready to use.

Canned high-volume veggies: mushrooms, asparagus

Frozen high-volume veggies (individual or mixed): mushrooms, zucchini, yellow squash, asparagus, cauliflower, kale

Packaged finds! Bagged cole slaw mix, a.k.a. shredded cabbage. Also common? Bags of ready-to-use chopped kale and spinach. Yum!

If a meal calls for raw chicken . . .
Buy precooked kinds—the less sodium the better. Look for fresh or frozen strips, cutlets, and chopped chicken. Or cook up a bunch of chicken in advance (see page 110), and use it for days. Here's a handy conversion chart . . .

If it calls for . . .	Use this . . .
4 ounces raw	3 ounces cooked
6 ounces raw	5 ounces cooked

DAY 4

BREAKFAST

8 ounces hot, room-temp, or cold water

Choose one of the following:
* Mega Fruit 'n Yogurt Bowl (page 124)
* Egg Scramble & Bun (page 125)
* Growing Oatmeal B-fast (page 126)

LUNCH

8 ounces room-temp or cold water

Choose one of the following:
* Ginormous Salad with Chicken, Turkey, or Tuna (page 128)
* Super-Sized Sandwich Platter with Tuna, Turkey, or Chicken (page 131)
* Veggie 'n Bean Bowl with Side of Greek Yogurt (page 132)

DINNER

8 ounces room-temp or cold water

Choose one of the following:
* HG-ified Fish or Chicken with Hot Veggies and Salad (page 134)
* Chicken Hungry Girlfredo Bowl (page 136)
* HG's Special Stir-Fry (page 138)

SNACKS

Choose any THREE snacks from the following:
* Grab-n-Go Snacks (page 188)
* Speedy Snacks (page 186)
* Snack Recipes (page 187)

Have each with 8 ounces room-temp or cold water.

More Time-Saving Shortcuts!

If a meal calls for chopped romaine or iceberg lettuce . . .
Use a bagged salad mix of pre-chopped greens. Extra veggies like carrots are perfectly fine, but make sure there are no fancy extras, like nuts or tortilla strips. If you're really in a hurry, hit a supermarket salad bar to assemble all the veggies for your salad!

If a meal calls for hard-boiled egg whites . . .
Make a whole batch of eggs at once, so you'll be able to just grab what you need when you need it. See page 109 for specific tips.

Or scramble them up instead. A serving of two large egg whites is equal to 1/4 cup egg whites or fat-free liquid egg substitute. In a microwave-safe mug sprayed with nonstick spray, microwave egg whites/substitute for 1 minute. Stir and microwave for 30 seconds, or until set. Or just scramble in a skillet sprayed with nonstick spray. Season with spices like garlic powder, onion powder, and black pepper.

Hot Tip! Snack Before Breakfast . . .

Don't want a big meal first thing in the a.m.? Start your day with one of your snacks, like 100 calories' worth of fruit or a light string cheese with 1/4 ounce of nuts. Then enjoy your breakfast midmorning. This could help you feel fuller throughout the day, too. It's what I typically do, and it works like a charm.

Food Cues: The Truth About Bread

I generally don't eat a lot of bread, because bread (any kind!) is a trigger food for me—it makes me crave MORE starchy foods. If this isn't the case for you, enjoy bread regularly while on the plan. Some people find a giant sandwich at lunch or a bun with butter at breakfast *very* satisfying. I bring this up in case you aren't even aware that bread (and other starchy carbs) MIGHT make you hungrier. Now that you know, pay attention, and see how it affects you. Then make your food decisions accordingly.

DAY 5

BREAKFAST

8 ounces hot, room-temp, or cold water

Choose one of the following:
* Mega Fruit 'n Yogurt Bowl (page 124)
* Egg Scramble & Bun (page 125)
* Growing Oatmeal B-fast (page 126)

LUNCH

8 ounces room-temp or cold water

Choose one of the following:
* Ginormous Salad with Chicken, Turkey, or Tuna (page 128)
* Super-Sized Sandwich Platter with Tuna, Turkey, or Chicken (page 131)
* Veggie 'n Bean Bowl with Side of Greek Yogurt (page 132)

DINNER

8 ounces room-temp or cold water

Choose one of the following:
* HG-ified Fish or Chicken with Hot Veggies and Salad (page 134)
* Chicken Hungry Girlfredo Bowl (page 136)
* HG's Special Stir-Fry (page 138)

SNACKS

Choose any THREE snacks from the following:
* Grab-n-Go Snacks (page 188)
* Speedy Snacks (page 186)
* Snack Recipes (page 187)

Have each with 8 ounces room-temp or cold water.

Extra, Extra! (Coffee Creamer, Ketchup & More)

You may be wondering how to factor in those little extras you just can't live without: milk in your coffee, ketchup on your eggs, a few hard candies . . . whatever it may be. Here's the deal. Since weight loss is all about calories in versus calories out, you can't *not* count them. So if you know you're going to have them, set a 50-calorie limit for the entire day. Then *halve* one of your three daily snacks. So instead of 2 cups halved strawberries for a snack, have 1 cup. Or instead of a whole 100-calorie bag of 94% fat-free microwave popcorn, have half a bag. And be extra-vigilant about measuring and counting those extras.

Lunch & Dinner Swap-a-rama!

Want to pack a Chicken Hungry Girlfredo Bowl to reheat on your lunch break and enjoy a Ginormous Salad for dinner? Feel like having HG-ified Chicken with Hot Veggies and Salad in the afternoon and then digging into a Super-Sized Sandwich Platter after work? Go for it! You can switch up lunch and dinner any day of the week.

Download The Hungry Girl Diet App to create custom shopping lists and track your food! Visit hungry-girl.com/diet for details.

DAY 6

BREAKFAST

8 ounces hot, room-temp, or cold water

Choose one of the following:
* Mega Fruit 'n Yogurt Bowl (page 124)
* Egg Scramble & Bun (page 125)
* Growing Oatmeal B-fast (page 126)

LUNCH

8 ounces room-temp or cold water

Choose one of the following:
* Ginormous Salad with Chicken, Turkey, or Tuna (page 128)
* Super-Sized Sandwich Platter with Tuna, Turkey, or Chicken (page 131)
* Veggie 'n Bean Bowl with Side of Greek Yogurt (page 132)

DINNER

8 ounces room-temp or cold water

Choose one of the following:
* HG-ified Fish or Chicken with Hot Veggies and Salad (page 134)
* Chicken Hungry Girlfredo Bowl (page 136)
* HG's Special Stir-Fry (page 138)

SNACKS

Choose any THREE snacks from the following:
* Grab-n-Go Snacks (page 188)
* Speedy Snacks (page 186)
* Snack Recipes (page 187)

Have each with 8 ounces room-temp or cold water.

HG FYI: Don't miss the budget-friendly advice on pages 72 and 74!

Secrets of Successful HG Dieters:
Trying New Things

I had never had broccoli cole slaw, but have found out that I really like it! It tastes really good and a lot like pasta . . . I had never had jicama before, but found it tastes good.
—Julie K. (lost 22 pounds)

I liked trying new foods that I would have never tried . . . I have found new foods that I would add to my regular diet.
—Rachael D. (lost 12 pounds)

I learned to try new fruits and vegetables that now are incorporated into my daily life.
—Nancy C. (lost 8.4 pounds)

DAY 7

BREAKFAST

8 ounces hot, room-temp, or cold water

Choose one of the following:
  * Mega Fruit 'n Yogurt Bowl (page 124)
  * Egg Scramble & Bun (page 125)
  * Growing Oatmeal B-fast (page 126)

LUNCH

8 ounces room-temp or cold water

Choose one of the following:
  * Ginormous Salad with Chicken, Turkey, or Tuna (page 128)
  * Super-Sized Sandwich Platter with Tuna,
    Turkey, or Chicken (page 131)
  * Veggie 'n Bean Bowl with Side of Greek Yogurt (page 132)

DINNER

8 ounces room-temp or cold water

Choose one of the following:
  * HG-ified Fish or Chicken with Hot Veggies and Salad (page 134)
  * Chicken Hungry Girlfredo Bowl (page 136)
  * HG's Special Stir-Fry (page 138)

SNACKS

Choose any THREE snacks from the following:
  * Grab-n-Go Snacks (page 188)
  * Speedy Snacks (page 186)
  * Snack Recipes (page 187)

Have each with 8 ounces room-temp or cold water.

WEEK 2

Congratulations on making it through Week 1!

Establishing new habits is the hard part, and you've made it over that hurdle. And get excited, because the next few weeks include SO many more meal options . . .

Weigh in at this point to check your progress. Remember to get on the scale at around the same time of day and in similar clothing as you did at the start of Week 1. If you lost weight, congratulations! This means you're doing a great job of sticking to the plan. Keep it up! If you haven't lost weight, a few factors could be to blame. See How to Avoid Common Missteps on the next page for helpful tips to get you on the weight-loss bandwagon. This diet works if you stick to it. So be super-vigilant, and you WILL see results.

Just like Week 1, you'll get three meals and three snacks on each day of the plan. If you have 75 pounds or more to lose, have a vigorous exercise routine, or feel the approximate 1,300-calorie level is too aggressive for you, consider adding one of the supplemental snacks found on page 220.

In addition to the Week 1 classics, you'll be given two more options for every meal each day this week! There are new spins on the staples (Oatmeal bowls! Huge salads!) as well as all-new craving-busting creations (Tacos! Chicken Parm!). These can all be found starting on page 140. Remember, you can continue to enjoy ANY and ALL of the Week 1 meals during Weeks 2 through 4. So if you have a favorite and/or find these to be easy options, go for it! The time-saving alternatives are especially helpful for busy days.

You can also switch up lunch and dinner any day of the week. If you'd prefer to have Day 1's Sloppy Jane Stir-Fry lunch in the evening and the Sesame-Ginger Salmon & Veggies dinner in the afternoon, do it.

The daily meal plans are meant to provide you with lots of variety, decadent options, and an easy-to-follow outline for weight loss. However, since ALL of the breakfasts and the lunch and dinner meals on the plan are similarly balanced, **you can choose to mix 'n match them however you like**! So if you love Day 2's Chicken So Low Mein with Side Salad and want to have it again on Day 4, you absolutely can.

Here we go!

How to Avoid Common Missteps

Measure carefully. Use measuring cups *and* a food scale. Be sure to measure or weigh ALL ingredients, but especially calorie-dense ones like oil, nuts, and cheese.

Follow ingredient lists closely. There's a big difference in calories between regular bread and light bread. Standard ground beef has much more fat than extra-lean ground beef. Regular butter has twice the fat and calories as light whipped butter or light buttery spread. You get the idea! See the supermarket list on page 90 for brand suggestions.

Drink at least eight cups of water a day. You'll feel more energized and be less likely to make poor food decisions. Plus, we often think we're hungry when we're actually a little dehydrated. Drinking enough water can help you feel fuller longer.

Don't drink your calories. Coffee drinks, sweetened iced tea, juice . . . These things can add hundreds of calories to your daily intake and prevent weight loss. If you crave these types of drinks, look for zero-calorie alternatives. See page 24 for more info on beverages like these.

Keep track of every bite. Make sure you're not overlooking the occasional extras here and there. It may sound tedious, but food journaling WORKS. Be brutally honest, and write down EVERYTHING you eat daily.

Limit dining out. Not forever, but for the four weeks on this plan. Remember, when you dine out, you never know if your food was prepared exactly as it should be or if your serving sizes are spot-on. Hidden ingredients can easily find their way into your meal. You'll get the best weight-loss results if you prepare your own meals as often as possible on the plan. When you do dine out, stick to the guidelines starting on page 98.

DAY 1

BREAKFAST

8 ounces hot, room-temp, or cold water

Choose one of the following:
* Pumped-Up Protein Oatmeal (page 143)
* Knife & Fork Avocado Chicken B-fast Burrito (page 147)
* Any Week 1 Breakfast (page 123)

LUNCH

8 ounces room-temp or cold water

Choose one of the following:
* Chinese Chicken Salad (page 154)
* Sloppy Jane Stir-Fry (page 162)
* Any Week 1 Lunch (page 123)

DINNER

8 ounces room-temp or cold water

Choose one of the following:
* Crunchy Beef Tacos with Side Salad (page 166)
* Sesame-Ginger Salmon & Veggies (page 172)
* Any Week 1 Dinner (page 123)

SNACKS

Choose any THREE snacks from the following:
* Grab-n-Go Snacks (page 188)
* Speedy Snacks (page 186)
* Snack Recipes (page 187)

Have each with 8 ounces room-temp or cold water.

Outsmart Your Trigger-Food Cravings!

Trigger foods are the ones that make you want more and more of them, potentially setting you off into an eating frenzy. (We've all been there!) For some, chocolate is a trigger food—one bite, and they can't stop eating chocolate all day. For me, it's chips, pretzels, and other carby, salty snacks. Give me a handful, and it's all over! Understanding your trigger foods is especially important when it comes to choosing your snacks on this plan. A low-fat fudge bar is a fantastic option for someone who can't stand the idea of life without chocolate. However, if a chocolate snack simply fuels your appetite for sweets rather than extinguishing it, I would recommend skipping it altogether. What are YOUR trigger foods? Think about it . . . Then make your snack selections accordingly!

DAY 2

BREAKFAST

8 ounces hot, room-temp, or cold water

Choose one of the following:
* Tropical Fruit 'n Yogurt Bowl (page 151)
* EggaMuffin B-fast (page 148)
* Any Week 1 Breakfast (page 123)

LUNCH

8 ounces room-temp or cold water

Choose one of the following:
* Chicken So Low Mein with Side Salad (page 163)
* Veggie-rific Salad (page 156)
* Any Week 1 Lunch (page 123)

DINNER

8 ounces room-temp or cold water

Choose one of the following:
* Chicken Parm with Saucy Pasta Swap (page 182)
* Big Burger with Side Salad (page 160)
* Any Week 1 Dinner (page 123)

SNACKS

Choose any THREE snacks from the following:
* Grab-n-Go Snacks (page 188)
* Speedy Snacks (page 186)
* Snack Recipes (page 187)

Have each with 8 ounces room-temp or cold water.

Pssst . . . One of tomorrow's breakfast options is a chilled oatmeal parfait. To save time in the morning, cook your oatmeal tonight, and refrigerate it overnight.

Secrets of Successful HG Dieters: Planning Ahead

I loved cutting up fresh vegetables from the farmers' market . . . so they were at the ready when I walked in the door at night. I precooked my big burgers, taco meat, and chicken, so that I could walk in the door from a long day at work and eat within minutes.
—Michelle M. (lost 16 pounds)

I always made my oatmeal and yogurts the night before, then added the toppings like Fiber One, nuts, and fruit the next day at work. It was easier for me to stay on [track] because I was prepared.
—Lori F. (lost 12.6 pounds)

I ended up just making Tupperware containers of chopped veggies and then labeled each either high-fiber or high-volume, and measured from there.
—Donna F. (lost 8 pounds)

I love the HG EggaMuffin. I made like seven at a time and froze them. It was perfect!
—Gary M. (lost 21.6 pounds)

DAY 3

BREAKFAST

8 ounces hot, room-temp, or cold water

Choose one of the following:
* Strawberry Peach Oatmeal Parfait (page 144)
* The Great Greek Egg Breakfast (page 150)
* Any Week 1 Breakfast (page 123)

LUNCH

8 ounces room-temp or cold water

Choose one of the following:
* Classic Chef Salad (page 158)
* Faux-Fried Chicken Strips with Side Salad (page 180)
* Any Week 1 Lunch (page 123)

DINNER

8 ounces room-temp or cold water

Choose one of the following:
* Balsamic BBQ Chicken with Side Salad (page 176)
* Ginormous Tofu Stir-Fry (page 168)
* Any Week 1 Dinner (page 123)

SNACKS

Choose any THREE snacks from the following:
* Grab-n-Go Snacks (page 188)
* Speedy Snacks (page 186)
* Snack Recipes (page 187)

Have each with 8 ounces room-temp or cold water.

Secrets of Successful HG Dieters:
Having All the Water . . . and Then Some

I drank all my water every day and sometimes even more than listed.
—Terri V. (lost 15 pounds)

I had a half-gallon pitcher I filled twice each day. I drank it all.
—Jenny H. (lost 8 pounds)

I am now addicted to water. I drink at least eight glasses, more if I get a workout in!!!
—Kier O. (lost 9 pounds)

Get Portion Savvy!

Face it: There *will* be times when you won't have a food scale or measuring cups—at restaurants, lunch meetings, etc. But if you pay close attention to portion sizes when you do weigh and measure everything, you'll be able to eyeball those servings pretty accurately when you don't have that scale handy. Test yourself! Next time you make your ginormous salad, first try to estimate 4 ounces of turkey or chicken. Then pop it on the scale to see how you did.

DAY 4

BREAKFAST

8 ounces hot, room-temp, or cold water

Choose one of the following:
* Berry Madness Yogurt Bowl (page 152)
* Veggie-Packed Egg Mug B-fast (page 149)
* Any Week 1 Breakfast (page 123)

LUNCH

8 ounces room-temp or cold water

Choose one of the following:
* BBQ Chicken Salad (page 155)
* Tuna Melt with Side Salad (page 164)
* Any Week 1 Lunch (page 123)

DINNER

8 ounces room-temp or cold water

Choose one of the following:
* Pizza-fied Chicken with Saucy Spaghetti Swap (page 170)
* Fajita Salad (page 157)
* Any Week 1 Dinner (page 123)

SNACKS

Choose any THREE snacks from the following:
* Grab-n-Go Snacks (page 188)
* Speedy Snacks (page 186)
* Snack Recipes (page 187)

Have each with 8 ounces room-temp or cold water.

HG FYI: Concerned about sodium? There's lots of helpful information on page 106.

Three-Step Plan for Obliterating Hunger!

I'll be honest: It's unlikely you'll find yourself hungry on this plan—especially once you're a few days in—because the meals and snacks are all very large and filling. But in case you do, here's how to handle it . . .

1. Remember, if you're not eating all the food in each meal, you CAN (and should) save it for later that day. So if you find yourself feeling hungry, eat those leftover berries from breakfast or the rest of that HUGE salad from lunch.

2. Have a tall glass of water. Slightly boring advice, but VERY effective. It's common to confuse thirst with hunger, so drink up! If you find cold water tough to get down, try some room-temp H_2O. Then wait five to ten minutes to let the water do its thing.

3. If you've done the above and still feel hungry, you may want to have one of the supplemental snacks found on page 220. These snacks are particularly helpful for those who have 75 pounds or more to lose, exercise vigorously, or simply find a 1,300-calorie target to be too aggressive.

DAY 5

BREAKFAST

8 ounces hot, room-temp, or cold water

Choose one of the following:
* Apple Walnut Oatmeal (page 145)
* Banana-Berry Yogurt Bowl (page 153)
* Any Week 1 Breakfast (page 123)

LUNCH

8 ounces room-temp or cold water

Choose one of the following:
* The HG Chop Chop (page 159)
* Sloppy Jane Stir-Fry (page 162)
* Any Week 1 Lunch (page 123)

DINNER

8 ounces room-temp or cold water

Choose one of the following:
* Chicken Fajita Tostadas (page 174)
* Chicken So Low Mein with Side Salad (page 163)
* Any Week 1 Dinner (page 123)

SNACKS

Choose any THREE snacks from the following:
* Grab-n-Go Snacks (page 188)
* Speedy Snacks (page 186)
* Snack Recipes (page 187)

Have each with 8 ounces room-temp or cold water.

Dining Out at a Glance

Yes, you'll get the best weight-loss results by prepping your own meals as often as you can, but it's entirely possible to eat at restaurants while on this plan. Here's a quick guide to plan-friendly meals. Don't miss the full Dining Out section on page 98!

HG Tip! Before you head out to a restaurant, check out the menu online. Then decide in advance exactly what you'll have. This is much better than showing up hungry and scrambling to make a smart choice.

Another HG Tip! Carry around a portion-controlled stash of almonds or pistachios. Not only are they great for emergency-snack situations (more on Emergency Snacks on page 56), but they're also perfect as part of a fruit and yogurt breakfast on the go.

Breakfast . . .

Fruit and Yogurt: If fat-free Greek yogurt isn't available, go with 6 ounces of any fat-free yogurt. Pair it with a large piece of fruit or fruit salad and 1/2 ounce of almonds or pistachios (about 12 almonds or 24 pistachios). Easy and delicious!

Egg-White or Egg Beaters Omelette: Request no cheese, plenty of veggies, and that it be prepared with little to no oil or butter. Get an English muffin or one slice of whole-wheat toast, and spread with a small amount of jam instead of butter. Add a small piece of fruit or fruit salad, and you've got a guilt-free morning meal.

Lunch and Dinner . . .

Salad with Chicken or Turkey: Keep it simple, and skip the croutons, cheese, and crunchy toppings. Stick with lots of greens and fresh veggies with a palm-sized serving of lean poultry. Ask for either oil and vinegar or low-fat/light dressing on the side, and use sparingly. (Dip, don't pour.) You can get this meal almost anywhere.

Fish or Chicken with Salad and Hot Veggies: Start with a side salad (same guidelines as above). Have your protein baked, broiled, or grilled and prepared dry or with very little oil. Order steamed veggies. (Get double veggies if the meal normally comes with pasta or a starchy side.). Add a squeeze of lemon for extra flavor.

DAY 6

BREAKFAST

8 ounces hot, room-temp, or cold water

Choose one of the following:
* Blueberry Almond Oatmeal (page 146)
* Tropical Fruit 'n Yogurt Bowl (page 151)
* Any Week 1 Breakfast (page 123)

LUNCH

8 ounces room-temp or cold water

Choose one of the following:
* Fajita Salad (page 157)
* Balsamic BBQ Chicken with Side Salad (page 176)
* Any Week 1 Lunch (page 123)

DINNER

8 ounces room-temp or cold water

Choose one of the following:
* Grilled Cheese Platter (page 173)
* Crunchy Beef Tacos with Side Salad (page 166)
* Any Week 1 Dinner (page 123)

SNACKS

Choose any THREE snacks from the following:
* Grab-n-Go Snacks (page 188)
* Speedy Snacks (page 186)
* Snack Recipes (page 187)

Have each with 8 ounces room-temp or cold water.

Pssst . . . One of tomorrow's breakfast options is a chilled oatmeal parfait. To save time in the morning, cook your oatmeal tonight, and refrigerate it overnight.

Craving-Busting Super Snacks!

Who says you can't indulge in favorites like pizza and French fries when on a diet? Not me!

If you're craving something hot and cheesy, have . . .
Easy Cheesy Noodles! (page 200)
Cheesy Faux-tato Skins! (page 208)
A Perfect Pizza-bella! (page 211)

If you're craving chocolate, have . . .
A Vitalicious VitaTop!
Chocolate-Chip-Stuffed Strawberries! (page 217)
A Fiber One 90 Calorie Brownie!
A low-fat frozen fudge pop with 100 calories or less
    (Enlightened bars are my top pick here)!
Cannoli Bites! (page 219)

If you're craving French fries, have . . .
Snack-tastic Butternut Fries! (page 209)
Easy Baked Carrot Fries! (page 210)

If you're craving chips or popcorn, have . . .
Baked Kale Chips! (page 200)
D.I.Y. Tortilla Chips! (page 212)
A 100-calorie bag of baked chips, popped chips, or
    tortilla chips (like Popchips or Kettle Brand Bakes)!
A 100-calorie bag of 94% fat-free microwave popcorn!

If you're craving pie or pastries, have . . .
An Upside-Down Cream Pie! (page 201)
Apple Pie in a Mug! (page 203)
A 6-ounce container of dessert-inspired fat-free yogurt
    (like Yoplait Light Apple Turnover)!
An Upside-Down Strawberry Pie! (page 213)

DAY 7

BREAKFAST

8 ounces hot, room-temp, or cold water

Choose one of the following:
- * Veggie-Packed Egg Mug B-fast (page 149)
- * Strawberry Peach Oatmeal Parfait (page 144)
- * Any Week 1 Breakfast (page 123)

LUNCH

8 ounces room-temp or cold water

Choose one of the following:
- * Classic Chef Salad (page 158)
- * Big Burger with Side Salad (page 160)
- * Any Week 1 Lunch (page 123)

DINNER

8 ounces room-temp or cold water

Choose one of the following:
- * Sesame-Ginger Salmon & Veggies (page 172)
- * Chicken Parm with Saucy Pasta Swap (page 182)
- * Any Week 1 Dinner (page 123)

SNACKS

Choose any THREE snacks from the following:
- * Grab-n-Go Snacks (page 188)
- * Speedy Snacks (page 186)
- * Snack Recipes (page 187)

Have each with 8 ounces room-temp or cold water.

WEEK 3

Way to go!

You're halfway through the four-week jump-start plan. That's quite an accomplishment! Kudos to you, if you've been staying on track. And if you haven't exactly been perfect, there's still time to step it up. You've got two full weeks left—plenty of time to see major results.

It's time to weigh in again to check your progress. Remember to get on the scale at around the same time of day as in previous weeks and in similar clothing. Heads up! If you had a big loss in the first week, you may experience a smaller loss this week. That's completely normal, so don't be discouraged. Just keep on the path, and you'll continue to drop pounds. If you didn't lose weight this week, revisit the How to Avoid Common Missteps section on page 40. And recommit yourself to the plan, starting NOW.

Week 3 is a fantastic time to really push yourself and follow the diet as closely as possible. The most successful Hungry Girl Diet followers prepare their own meals on a daily basis and keep dining out to a minimum while on the plan. Now is also a good time to add some physical activity to your routine. If you're already exercising, take it to the next level. Increase the length of your workouts or step up the intensity. If you haven't been active, think about starting now. Pick up a workout DVD, or call a friend to join you for daily jogs or brisk walks. For more exercise ideas—including ideas for beginners—visit page 112.

Before you dive into the second half of the plan, here are three important reminders:

1. The daily meal plans are designed to give you an easy guide to weight loss, packed with variety and indulgence. But you can mix 'n match meals however you like. So feel free to repeat favorites and swap lunches with dinners. And don't forget about the Week 1 meals . . . They're incredible staples that can and should be enjoyed throughout the plan.

2. In addition to having at least 8 ounces of water with each meal and snack, drink another 16 ounces (or more) throughout the day. It's common to confuse thirst for hunger, so keep up with your water intake and you'll feel more satisfied.

3. If you have 75 pounds or more to lose, have a vigorous exercise routine, or feel the approximate 1,300-calorie level is too aggressive for you, consider adding one of the supplemental snacks found on page 220. However, if you've been eating the additional snacks throughout the first half of the plan, you may want to challenge yourself and go without them for the remainder of the plan. This could really kick your weight loss into high gear. Give it a try, and see how you feel!

Here's to an amazing third week! Enjoy . . .

Emergency Snack 101

Cheesy cliché alert: If you fail to plan, you plan to fail. It's true! So keep appropriate snacks on hand at all times . . .

In your purse, backpack, gym bag, etc.:
100-calorie pack of almonds
100-calorie snack bar (like Fiber One Protein)
200-calorie snack bar (like Quest Bar; have in place of
 two snacks, either at once or half at a time)

In your desk drawer:
100-calorie pouches of low-sodium tuna packed in water
Whole fruit (a medium pear, apple, or banana)
100-calorie bags of freeze-dried fruit
100-calorie bags of 94% fat-free microwave popcorn

In your office fridge:
Light string cheese (to pair with fruit or nuts)
6-ounce containers of fat-free yogurt (flavored regular or
 plain Greek)
No-salt-added turkey breast with cucumber
Cut veggies with dip
Cut fruit

See the Grab-n-Go Snacks section on page 188 *for more
need-to-know snack info!*

**For more tools
for success—including
an app that lets you create
custom shopping lists and
track your food—visit
hungry-girl.com/diet!**

DAY 1

BREAKFAST

8 ounces hot, room-temp, or cold water

Choose one of the following:
* EggaMuffin B-fast (page 148)
* Pumped-Up Protein Oatmeal (page 143)
* Any Week 1 Breakfast (page 123)

LUNCH

8 ounces room-temp or cold water

Choose one of the following:
* Veggie-rific Salad (page 156)
* Pizza-fied Chicken with Saucy Spaghetti Swap (page 170)
* Any Week 1 Lunch or Dinner (page 123)

DINNER

8 ounces room-temp or cold water

Choose one of the following:
* Ginormous Tofu Stir-Fry (page 168)
* BBQ Chicken Salad (page 155)
* Any Week 1 Lunch or Dinner (page 123)

SNACKS

Choose any THREE snacks from the following:
* Grab-n-Go Snacks (page 188)
* Speedy Snacks (page 186)
* Snack Recipes (page 187)

Have each with 8 ounces room-temp or cold water.

How to Handle a Slip . . .

No one's perfect. Not me, not you, not ANYONE. So don't let a bad food decision derail the whole diet, and do NOT beat yourself up over it. You're only human. So get over it, and move on . . .

Some people use a slip as an excuse to continue overindulging, causing a snowball effect that's hard to rebound from. If you eat too much or have a high-calorie meal, there's no reason to give up and blow the rest of the day. That kind of attitude is not productive and could lead you to blow the week or even the MONTH.

Don't starve or restrict yourself to make up for a misstep. That'll only make things worse, since your body will be thrown off by the two extremes. And dipping below 1,200 calories per day is never recommended and could curtail your weight loss. The best way to get back on track is to start following the plan again immediately—as in, at YOUR NEXT MEAL OR SNACK.

Secrets of Successful HG Dieters: Water with Lemon

I drank the lemon water constantly. I keep a water kettle next to my desk at work, and I drink several mugs of water each day.
—Michelle M. (lost 16 pounds)

I really believe this is the key, and I did it daily. I'm up to drinking four to five big bottles of water with lemon a day and honestly feel better . . .
—Colleen M. (lost 14.5 pounds)

DAY 2

BREAKFAST

8 ounces hot, room-temp, or cold water

Choose one of the following:
* Berry Madness Yogurt Bowl (page 152)
* Knife & Fork Avocado Chicken B-fast Burrito (page 147)
* Any Week 1 Breakfast (page 123)

LUNCH

8 ounces room-temp or cold water

Choose one of the following:
* Chinese Chicken Salad (page 154)
* Chicken Fajita Tostadas (page 174)
* Any Week 1 Lunch or Dinner (page 123)

DINNER

8 ounces room-temp or cold water

Choose one of the following:
* Faux-Fried Chicken Strips with Side Salad (page 180)
* Tuna Melt with Side Salad (page 164)
* Any Week 1 Lunch or Dinner (page 123)

SNACKS

Choose any THREE snacks from the following:
* Grab-n-Go Snacks (page 188)
* Speedy Snacks (page 186)
* Snack Recipes (page 187)

Have each with 8 ounces room-temp or cold water.

HG Reminder: Dining out? Don't wing it! Visit page 98 for all the need-to-know info.

Calorie-Free Flavor-Uppers!

Personalize any meal with these virtually calorie-free enhancers . . .

Red pepper flakes—I'm a fan of spicy foods. They taste great, stop me from overeating (because of how hot they are!), and make me drink more water. These flakes are especially good with Italian and Asian-inspired meals. Careful though—they pack a punch!

Onion powder, garlic powder, and chili powder—What's great about these staple spices is that they're foolproof. They won't completely alter the taste of a dish; they'll just give it more flavor. I add them to egg mugs and stir-frys all the time.

Salt-free seasoning mixes—Many meals on this plan call for cooking with salt-free seasoning mix, like Mrs. Dash Original Blend. It easily transforms plain chicken or fish into something completely amazing, and without adding *any* sodium! Have some fun with all the different versions on store shelves. Lemon pepper, Southwest, garlic and herb . . . Try some sprinkled on steamed veggies, too. Really GREAT!

Fresh basil, cilantro, or other herbs—I LOVE fresh herbs. They make everything taste better. Sprinkle basil over your Chicken Hungry Girlfredo Bowl (page 136); add some cilantro to your tacos (page 166) or the Fajita Salad (page 157); or zazzle up tuna sandwiches (page 131 and 164) with fresh dill!

Lemon or lime juice—Citrus juice will brighten up the flavor of your meal. Most of us have squeezed a lemon wedge over a piece of fish—a classic combo—but try a little lemon or lime juice over salads, steamed veggies . . . even fruit!

DAY 3

BREAKFAST

8 ounces hot, room-temp, or cold water

Choose one of the following:
  * Apple Walnut Oatmeal (page 145)
  * The Great Greek Egg Breakfast (page 150)
  * Any Week 1 Breakfast (page 123)

LUNCH

8 ounces room-temp or cold water

Choose one of the following:
  * The HG Chop Chop (page 159)
  * Chicken So Low Mein with Side Salad (page 163)
  * Any Week 1 Lunch or Dinner (page 123)

DINNER

8 ounces room-temp or cold water

Choose one of the following:
  * Fruity Fish & Potato Foil Pack with Side Salad (page 178)
  * Chicken Parm with Saucy Pasta Swap (page 182)
  * Any Week 1 Lunch or Dinner (page 123)

SNACKS

Choose any THREE snacks from the following:
  * Grab-n-Go Snacks (page 188)
  * Speedy Snacks (page 186)
  * Snack Recipes (page 187)

Have each with 8 ounces room-temp or cold water.

Five-Minute Supermarket Meals

Think you don't have time to throw together an HG-diet-plan-friendly lunch or dinner? Guess again! With a few pantry staples at home, you can just walk into a supermarket and grab . . .

Frozen stir-fry veggies, frozen broccoli florets, a bottle of sauce with 25 calories or less per 1-tablespoon serving (Lawry's Santa Fe Chili Marinade is one of my favorites!), and precooked skinless chicken breast. Nuke 2 cups stir-fry veggies with 1 ½ cups broccoli. Add 4 ounces chicken, 2 tablespoons sauce, and a teaspoon of oil. Heat and eat!

A 16-ounce bag of mixed lettuce, a 5-ounce can of low-sodium tuna packed in water, bagged sugar snap peas, sliced mushrooms, and canned black beans. Measure out a cup each snap peas and mushrooms and ¼ cup beans. Drain the tuna and rinse the beans, and toss it all with 1 ½ tablespoons vinegar and 1 teaspoon oil. Salad perfection!

A steamable 12-ounce bag of broccoli cole slaw, a tub of light sour cream, a wheel of The Laughing Cow Light cheese wedges, and a package of precooked skinless chicken breast. Steam your slaw, and stir in 2 cheese wedges and 2 tablespoons sour cream. Nuke until melted, stir, and add 4 ounces chicken. Season with garlic powder and paprika, if you like. Girlfredo goodness!

A pack of 100-calorie flat sandwich buns or light bread and 4 ounces no-salt-added turkey breast. Hit the salad bar to get lettuce and tomato for your sandwich, plus a 2-cup side salad of lettuce, tomato, and mushrooms. When you get home, assemble the sandwich, spread it with 2 teaspoons light mayo, and toss the salad with 2 ½ teaspoons vinegar and ½ teaspoon oil. Easy and excellent!

DAY 4

BREAKFAST

8 ounces hot, room-temp, or cold water

Choose one of the following:
   * Banana-Berry Yogurt Bowl (page 153)
   * Blueberry Almond Oatmeal (page 146)
   * Any Week 1 Breakfast (page 123)

LUNCH

8 ounces room-temp or cold water

Choose one of the following:
   * BBQ Chicken Salad (page 155)
   * Sloppy Jane Stir-Fry (page 162)
   * Any Week 1 Lunch or Dinner (page 123)

DINNER

8 ounces room-temp or cold water

Choose one of the following:
   * Grilled Cheese Platter (page 173)
   * Balsamic BBQ Chicken with Side Salad (page 176)
   * Any Week 1 Lunch or Dinner (page 123)

SNACKS

Choose any THREE snacks from the following:
   * Grab-n-Go Snacks (page 188)
   * Speedy Snacks (page 186)
   * Snack Recipes (page 187)

Have each with 8 ounces room-temp or cold water.

Pssst . . . One of tomorrow's breakfast options is a chilled oatmeal parfait. To save time in the morning, cook your oatmeal tonight, and refrigerate it overnight.

Secrets of Successful HG Dieters:
Incorporating Week 1 Meals Throughout the Plan

I would use the newer recipes off and on, but when I found one I liked, I stuck with it. For example, the Girlfredo Bowl. I used that one A LOT.
—Amy D. (lost 10.2 pounds)

I mixed it up. I felt the Week 1 meals were so easy that I gravitated toward them, especially for lunch.
—Gary M. (lost 21.6 pounds)

I went back to the Week 1 meals when I didn't feel like making the meals that were offered for a particular day or if I just didn't feel like "cooking." They were easy to prepare.
—Donna F. (lost 8 pounds)

I did some of both. I liked the burger, fajitas, and Chinese chicken salad a lot, but I also found the Girlfredo Bowl and sandwich platters delicious.
—Emily R. (lost 7.5 pounds)

DAY 5

BREAKFAST

8 ounces hot, room-temp, or cold water

Choose one of the following:
   * Strawberry Peach Oatmeal Parfait (page 144)
   * EggaMuffin B-fast (page 148)
   * Any Week 1 Breakfast (page 123)

LUNCH

8 ounces room-temp or cold water

Choose one of the following:
   * Chinese Chicken Salad (page 154)
   * Sesame-Ginger Salmon & Veggies (page 172)
   * Any Week 1 Lunch or Dinner (page 123)

DINNER

8 ounces room-temp or cold water

Choose one of the following:
   * Pizza-fied Chicken with Saucy Spaghetti Swap (page 170)
   * Ginormous Tofu Stir-Fry (page 168)
   * Any Week 1 Lunch or Dinner (page 123)

SNACKS

Choose any THREE snacks from the following:
   * Grab-n-Go Snacks (page 188)
   * Speedy Snacks (page 186)
   * Snack Recipes (page 187)

Have each with 8 ounces room-temp or cold water.

Plan-Ahead Ideas! (Time-Saving Tips)

Chicken
Cook up a lot of chicken at once (see page 110), and use it for several days in meals that call for raw or cooked chicken.

If it calls for . . .	Use this . . .
4 ounces raw	3 ounces cooked
6 ounces raw	5 ounces cooked

Vegetables
Chop up your favorite veggies ahead of time, so they're ready to go when you need them. You can also find pre-chopped veggies in the produce section, both individual and mixed. Many meals on the plan call for high-fiber or high-volume vegetables, giving many options for each. (Full lists are on page 111.) So if you love red bell peppers and mushrooms, buy and chop a bunch and use them all week in lots of different meals.

Dressings
Make a big batch of your favorite HG dressing (recipes found on page 197), rather than preparing it at each meal.

Hard-Boiled Eggs
Cook a dozen eggs at once, so you'll have some on hand for whenever you need them. See page 109 for specific tips!

DAY 6

BREAKFAST

8 ounces hot, room-temp, or cold water

Choose one of the following:
* Knife & Fork Avocado Chicken B-fast Burrito (page 147)
* Tropical Fruit 'n Yogurt Bowl (page 151)
* Any Week 1 Breakfast (page 123)

LUNCH

8 ounces room-temp or cold water

Choose one of the following:
* Fajita Salad (page 157)
* Balsamic BBQ Chicken with Side Salad (page 176)
* Any Week 1 Lunch or Dinner (page 123)

DINNER

8 ounces room-temp or cold water

Choose one of the following:
* Big Burger with Side Salad (page 160)
* Chicken Fajita Tostadas (page 174)
* Any Week 1 Lunch or Dinner (page 123)

SNACKS

Choose any THREE snacks from the following:
* Grab-n-Go Snacks (page 188)
* Speedy Snacks (page 186)
* Snack Recipes (page 187)

Have each with 8 ounces room-temp or cold water.

HG FYI: Craving a cocktail? Check out the Happy Hour section on page 78 and the margarita recipe on page 216!

Packed-Lunch Pointers

Top Tips!
Pack your afternoon meal in an insulated lunch bag so that your lunch stays cool during your commute. Then refrigerate it once you get to the office. No fridge? Toss a heavy-duty ice pack in with your lunch.

Sandwiches
Lightly toast your bread or bun to avoid a soggy situation. You can also pack any high-moisture ingredients (like tomato slices and tuna salad) separately, and assemble them at lunchtime.

Salads
Put all ingredients *except* dressing in a large sealable container. Pack the dressing separately, or store a bottle with your name on it in the office fridge.

Stir-Frys, Noodle Bowls, and More Hot Meals
Prepare these the night before, allow them to cool, and refrigerate in microwave-safe containers with lids. Pack 'em up, and microwave at work. Some can even be enjoyed chilled . . . It totally depends on what your personal preferences are!

DAY 7

BREAKFAST

8 ounces hot, room-temp, or cold water

Choose one of the following:
   * Pumped-Up Protein Oatmeal (page 143)
   * Berry Madness Yogurt Bowl (page 152)
   * Any Week 1 Breakfast (page 123)

LUNCH

8 ounces room-temp or cold water

Choose one of the following:
   * Veggie-rific Salad (page 156)
   * Chicken Parm with Saucy Pasta Swap (page 182)
   * Any Week 1 Lunch or Dinner (page 123)

DINNER

8 ounces room-temp or cold water

Choose one of the following:
   * Crunchy Beef Tacos with Side Salad (page 166)
   * Fruity Fish & Potato Foil Pack with Side Salad (page 178)
   * Any Week 1 Lunch or Dinner (page 123)

SNACKS

Choose any THREE snacks from the following:
   * Grab-n-Go Snacks (page 188)
   * Speedy Snacks (page 186)
   * Snack Recipes (page 187)

Have each with 8 ounces room-temp or cold water.

WEEK 4

Congratulations!
You are in the HOMESTRETCH!

It's truly an accomplishment to stick to *any* weight-loss plan for this long, and whether or not you're doing it perfectly, you're DOING it. (But I sincerely hope you're sticking to the plan, because you WILL see great results!)

It's time again to hop on the scale to see how you're progressing. Broken-record alert: Weigh in at about the same time of day as in earlier weeks and in similar clothes. If you've been sticking to the plan, chances are you're looking at an impressive week of weight loss. AWESOME. If your eating wasn't perfect during the past week, don't beat yourself up or throw in the towel. You have an entire week to turn things around, and you can always extend the plan or repeat it to continue losing weight.

What's different about Week 4? While you still have carefully crafted meal plans at your fingertips, this week gives you complete freedom to choose from ALL the breakfasts, lunches, and dinners found throughout this book. So revisit favorites or try something completely new and different.

Remember, planning is one of the keys to successful dieting. So look ahead at the meal suggestions, and decide what you want to have for the next several days. Then hit the supermarket to stock up! If you feel like changing things up a little this week, pick up a few new salt-free seasoning mixes and low-calorie sauces, marinades, and salad dressings. These can totally transform the flavor of many meals on the plan.

Wanna REALLY maximize your weight-loss results this week? Skip dining out altogether. It's only one week, and you can do pretty much anything for just one week! This will ensure your daily calorie count is exactly where it should be for weight loss. And challenge yourself to get in a little extra exercise this week as well. Flip to Hungry Girl's Guide to Exercise on page 112 for some ideas.

Hope you're hungry, because Week 4 starts in three, two, one . . .

Budget-Friendly Advice

Top Tips!
Staples like fat-free Greek yogurt, old-fashioned oats, and nuts can be purchased in large multi-serving packages. For big bags of snacks (like baked chips), immediately break them down into single servings for portion control.

Wait for deals, and then stock up. Keep an eye out for special offers on frozen foods, foods that can be frozen, and foods with long shelf lives.

Collect coupons. Check out the Sunday paper, or seek them out online. There are SO many coupons available, from those found on money-saving sites to ones provided by food companies themselves. Some websites don't even require printing; they simply apply savings to your supermarket discount card.

Fruits and Vegetables
Choose seasonal produce, for both snacks and meals. There's generally a lot of whatever's in season, so stores lower the prices to sell it all while it's still fresh. And since many meals on the plan call for high-fiber or high-volume veggies, giving lots of options for each, you can choose the cheapest. Find the full lists on page 111.

Un-prepped vegetables like heads of celery, stem-on green beans, and unwashed lettuce are generally less expensive than ready-to-eat packaged varieties. Sure, they take a little extra time to prepare, but they'll save you some cash.

Frozen fruits and veggies can also be money savers. Stick with store brands, or just go for the most inexpensive packs. Check the ingredients to make sure nothing's been added.

DAY 1

BREAKFAST

8 ounces hot, room-temp, or cold water

Choose one of the following:
   * Veggie-Packed Egg Mug B-fast (page 149)
   * Tropical Fruit 'n Yogurt Bowl (page 151)
   * Any HG Diet Plan Breakfast (page 123 and 141)

LUNCH

8 ounces room-temp or cold water

Choose one of the following:
   * Classic Chef Salad (page 158)
   * Tuna Melt with Side Salad (page 164)
   * Any HG Diet Plan Lunch or Dinner (page 123 and 141)

DINNER

8 ounces room-temp or cold water

Choose one of the following:
   * Grilled Cheese Platter (page 173)
   * Chicken So Low Mein with Side Salad (page 163)
   * Any HG Diet Plan Lunch or Dinner (page 123 and 141)

SNACKS

Choose any THREE snacks from the following:
   * Grab-n-Go Snacks (page 188)
   * Speedy Snacks (page 186)
   * Snack Recipes (page 187)

Have each with 8 ounces room-temp or cold water.

More Budget-Friendly Advice

Meat and Seafood
Compare prices at the meat counter, fresh packaged section, and freezer aisle. You never know where the best deal might be. You can also stock up when there's a sale, and freeze it until you need it!

Bread
Store in the fridge or freezer to lengthen its shelf life.

Make the Most of Leftover Ingredients
Choose meal options by what ingredients you already have on hand. You can also use leftover ingredients in snacks. In fact, we specifically developed some snack recipes for this very purpose!

DAY 2

BREAKFAST

8 ounces hot, room-temp, or cold water

Choose one of the following:
* The Great Greek Egg Breakfast (page 150)
* Banana-Berry Yogurt Bowl (page 153)
* Any HG Diet Plan Breakfast (page 123 and 141)

LUNCH

8 ounces room-temp or cold water

Choose one of the following:
* The HG Chop Chop (page 159)
* Faux-Fried Chicken Strips with Side Salad (page 180)
* Any HG Diet Plan Lunch or Dinner (page 123 and 141)

DINNER

8 ounces room-temp or cold water

Choose one of the following:
* Sloppy Jane Stir-Fry (page 162)
* Fruity Fish & Potato Foil Pack with Side Salad (page 178)
* Any HG Diet Plan Lunch or Dinner (page 123 and 141)

SNACKS

Choose any THREE snacks from the following:
* Grab-n-Go Snacks (page 188)
* Speedy Snacks (page 186)
* Snack Recipes (page 187)

Have each with 8 ounces room-temp or cold water.

HG Reminder: Don't forget to have two additional 8-ounce glasses of water throughout the day!

Secrets of Successful HG Dieters: Limiting Dining Out, Following the Guide When They Do

I dined out only once. I stuck with the plan for the most part . . . Now I take a closer look at swaps when eating out.
—Nancy S. (lost 12.6 pounds)

I went out to eat three times while on the plan. I usually stuck to chicken or fish and veggies. I also would check the restaurant's website before ordering to get nutritional information.
—Rachael D. (lost 12 pounds)

When you learn how, it is even easy to eat out. Most restaurants have egg whites, salad, and grilled chicken. Heck, even the zoo had grilled chicken salad!
—Sharon R. (lost 8.8 pounds)

DAY 3

BREAKFAST

8 ounces hot, room-temp, or cold water

Choose one of the following:
   * Pumped-Up Protein Oatmeal (page 143)
   * EggaMuffin B-fast (page 148)
   * Any HG Diet Plan Breakfast (page 123 and 141)

LUNCH

8 ounces room-temp or cold water

Choose one of the following:
   * Pizza-fied Chicken with Saucy Spaghetti Swap (page 170)
   * Chinese Chicken Salad (page 154)
   * Any HG Diet Plan Lunch or Dinner (page 123 and 141)

DINNER

8 ounces room-temp or cold water

Choose one of the following:
   * Sesame-Ginger Salmon & Veggies (page 172)
   * Chicken Parm with Saucy Pasta Swap (page 182)
   * Any HG Diet Plan Lunch or Dinner (page 123 and 141)

SNACKS

Choose any THREE snacks from the following:
   * Grab-n-Go Snacks (page 188)
   * Speedy Snacks (page 186)
   * Snack Recipes (page 187)

Have each with 8 ounces room-temp or cold water.

Happy Hour

There's no reason you can't indulge in a cocktail while losing weight. Just make it a 100-calorie cocktail, and count it as one of your snacks. In fact, there's an easy (and amazing!) margarita recipe on page 216. Here are some more drinks that fit the 100-calorie bill . . .

A single-shot mixed drink with a zero-calorie mixer (1½ ounces rum, tequila, or vodka with diet soda or seltzer/club soda)

A bottle of light beer (100 calories or less)

5 ounces of champagne

4 ounces of wine

With the mixed drink, watch out for tonic water. Unless it's diet tonic, it has about as many calories and as much sugar as regular soda. As for wine, 4 ounces is smaller than the average glass. If you're at home, measure it out. If you're out and about, eyeball a ½-cup portion.

DAY 4

BREAKFAST

8 ounces hot, room-temp, or cold water

Choose one of the following:
* Knife & Fork Avocado Chicken B-fast Burrito (page 147)
* Apple Walnut Oatmeal (page 145)
* Any HG Diet Plan Breakfast (page 123 and 141)

LUNCH

8 ounces room-temp or cold water

Choose one of the following:
* Fajita Salad (page 157)
* Ginormous Tofu Stir-Fry (page 168)
* Any HG Diet Plan Lunch or Dinner (page 123 and 141)

DINNER

8 ounces room-temp or cold water

Choose one of the following:
* BBQ Chicken Salad (page 155)
* Crunchy Beef Tacos with Side Salad (page 166)
* Any HG Diet Plan Lunch or Dinner (page 123 and 141)

SNACKS

Choose any THREE snacks from the following:
* Grab-n-Go Snacks (page 188)
* Speedy Snacks (page 186)
* Snack Recipes (page 187)

Have each with 8 ounces room-temp or cold water.

HG Reminder: Dining out? Don't wing it! Visit page 98 for all the need-to-know info.

Plan for the Future!

Make a list (or bookmark) your favorite meals and snacks. They're great for continued weight loss and maintenance.

Test your ability to eyeball portion sizes. The better you can commit common serving sizes to memory, the easier it'll be to make smart decisions in the future.

And for everything else you need to know, flip to page 222 for Life After the Four-Week Plan! (Continued Weight Loss, Maintenance, and Survival Strategies.)

DAY 5

BREAKFAST

8 ounces hot, room-temp, or cold water

Choose one of the following:
   * Strawberry Peach Oatmeal Parfait (page 144)
   * Banana-Berry Yogurt Bowl (page 153)
   * Any HG Diet Plan Breakfast (page 123 and 141)

LUNCH

8 ounces room-temp or cold water

Choose one of the following:
   * Veggie-rific Salad (page 156)
   * Big Burger with Side Salad (page 160)
   * Any HG Diet Plan Lunch or Dinner (page 123 and 141)

DINNER

8 ounces room-temp or cold water

Choose one of the following:
   * Balsamic BBQ Chicken with Side Salad (page 176)
   * Tuna Melt with Side Salad (page 164)
   * Any HG Diet Plan Lunch or Dinner (page 123 and 141)

SNACKS

Choose any THREE snacks from the following:
   * Grab-n-Go Snacks (page 188)
   * Speedy Snacks (page 186)
   * Snack Recipes (page 187)

Have each with 8 ounces room-temp or cold water.

Secrets of Successful HG Dieters: Turning to Craving-Busting Swaps

I feel confident about going out to eat with friends and not being tempted by foods that they are eating. I know now that if I want something sweet, there are alternatives to Blizzards and cupcakes. I have fudge pops and VitaTops.
—Rachael D. (lost 12 pounds)

I loved the Chicken So Low Mein. Great Chinese alternative. And my staple, [Faux-Fried] Chicken Strips with Side Salad!!!!!
—Kier O. (lost 9 pounds)

Last week, my class had these brownies that smelled soooooo good, and I was able to resist while everyone around me was munching away because I knew I had a VitaTop in my freezer and I could toast it when I got home.
—Stevenie E. (lost 11 pounds)

I'm addicted to ice cream so my daily fudge bar rocked!
—Terri S. (lost 13.1 pounds)

DAY 6

BREAKFAST

8 ounces hot, room-temp, or cold water

Choose one of the following:

* Blueberry Almond Oatmeal (page 146)
* Veggie-Packed Egg Mug B-fast (page 149)
* Any HG Diet Plan Breakfast (page 123 and 141)

LUNCH

8 ounces room-temp or cold water

Choose one of the following:

* The HG Chop Chop (page 159)
* Chicken So Low Mein with Side Salad (page 163)
* Any HG Diet Plan Lunch or Dinner (page 123 and 141)

DINNER

8 ounces room-temp or cold water

Choose one of the following:

* Faux-Fried Chicken Strips with Side Salad (page 180)
* Fruity Fish & Potato Foil Pack with Side Salad (page 178)
* Any HG Diet Plan Lunch or Dinner (page 123 and 141)

SNACKS

Choose any THREE snacks from the following:

* Grab-n-Go Snacks (page 188)
* Speedy Snacks (page 186)
* Snack Recipes (page 187)

Have each with 8 ounces room-temp or cold water.

It's Almost the End of the Jump Start . . .
Time for a REWARD!

This doesn't mean it's time to go eat a huge pizza . . .
Celebrate your accomplishment in a non-food-capacity:

* Go shopping. It doesn't have to be a full spree, but buy
  yourself a few new pieces of clothing in honor of those
  pounds you've shed. Bonus: Shopping burns calories!

* Have a girls' (or guys') night in. Magical Margarita Lights
  (page 216) all around!

* Enjoy a spa treatment. Get a massage, a pedicure, a
  haircut . . . Whatever!

DAY 7

BREAKFAST

8 ounces hot, room-temp, or cold water

Choose one of the following:
* Berry Madness Yogurt Bowl (page 152)
* The Great Greek Egg Breakfast (page 150)
* Any HG Diet Plan Breakfast (page 123 and 141)

LUNCH

8 ounces room-temp or cold water

Choose one of the following:
* Classic Chef Salad (page 158)
* Sloppy Jane Stir-Fry (page 162)
* Any HG Diet Plan Lunch or Dinner (page 123 and 141)

DINNER

8 ounces room-temp or cold water

Choose one of the following:
* Pizza-fied Chicken with Saucy Spaghetti Swap (page 170)
* Sesame-Ginger Salmon & Veggies (page 172)
* Any HG Diet Plan Lunch or Dinner (page 123 and 141)

SNACKS

Choose any THREE snacks from the following:
* Grab-n-Go Snacks (page 188)
* Speedy Snacks (page 186)
* Snack Recipes (page 187)

Have each with 8 ounces room-temp or cold water.

CONGRATULATIONS!

You've finished the four-week plan.

You've lost weight, shed inches, dropped sizes, and are likely feeling GREAT! Wondering what's next? Flip to page 222 for Life After the Four-Week Plan! (Continued Weight Loss, Maintenance, and Survival Strategies)!

HUNGRY GIRL
DIET RESOURCES

SUPERMARKET LIST OF DIET-PLAN STAPLES

Since this plan provides you with a LOT of mix 'n match options, there isn't ONE shopping list that applies to everyone. These grocery-store staples should get you started, but you'll need to build your exact shopping list based on the meals you choose. Here are some recommended items, both generic and specific. Brand names are included when there is a specific company that makes an outstanding product.

Download The Hungry Girl Diet App to create custom shopping lists and track your food! Visit hungry-girl.com/diet for details.

DAIRY

Cheese

Light string cheese

The Laughing Cow Light cheese wedges

Yogurt

Fat-free plain Greek yogurt
    Fage Total 0%, Chobani 0%, Oikos 0%

Fat-free flavored yogurt (for snacking)
    Yoplait Light (and Yoplait Greek 100)
    Dannon Light & Fit (and Light & Fit Greek)

Egg Products

Fat-free liquid egg substitute
    Egg Beaters Original, Better'n Eggs, Nulaid ReddiEgg

Liquid egg whites
    AllWhites, Egg Beaters 100% Egg Whites

Eggs (for hard-boiled whites)

Milk

Fat-free milk

Butter

Light buttery spread and light whipped butter in a tub
    Brummel & Brown, Land O'Lakes, Smart Balance

A REFRIGERATED STAPLE

House Foods Tofu Shirataki Noodle Substitute (refrigerated tofu section!)

CEREAL

Cold Cereal

Fiber One Original bran cereal (or All-Bran Original)*

Fiber One is sweetened with aspartame. If you prefer a high-fiber cereal made without artificial sweeteners, use All-Bran Original.

Hot Cereal

Old-fashioned oats
    Quaker

POULTRY AND SEAFOOD

Poultry

Boneless skinless chicken breast (raw and/or precooked)

No-salt-added turkey breast (check the deli counter)
    Boars Head

Seafood

Tilapia, cod, and/or sea bass (fresh or frozen)

Canned and pouched low-sodium tuna packed in water
    StarKist

PRODUCE

Fresh Vegetables

High-fiber veggies (tomatoes, onions, bell peppers, green beans,
    sugar snap peas, snow peas, bean sprouts, broccoli, Brussels
    sprouts, carrots, jicama)

High-volume veggies (mushrooms, cucumbers, cabbage, celery,
    zucchini, eggplant, yellow squash, asparagus, cauliflower,
    kale, spinach)

Romaine or iceberg lettuce

Spaghetti squash

Bagged Produce

Lettuce mixes

Broccoli cole slaw

Frozen Vegetables

High-fiber veggies (peppers, green beans, sugar snap peas,
    snow peas, broccoli, Brussels sprouts, carrots)

High-volume veggies (mushrooms, asparagus, cauliflower, kale)

Fresh Fruit (Choose Your Favorites!)

Apples

Bananas

Blackberries

Blueberries

Cantaloupe

Cherries

Clementines (or other small mandarin oranges)

Grapes

Grapefruit

Honeydew melon

Lemons

Mangoes

Nectarines

Oranges

Peaches

Pears

Pineapple

Pomegranates (Look for 100-calorie containers of POM POMs, ready-to-eat arils!)

Raspberries

Strawberries

Tangerines (or other medium mandarin oranges)

Watermelon

Frozen Fruit (No Sugar Added)

Blackberries

Raspberries

Strawberries

And any other unsweetened fruit

CANNED FOODS

Pure pumpkin
    Libby's 100%

Black beans

Garbanzo beans (chickpeas)

Kidney beans

SNACKS

Crackers, Chips, and Other Crunchy Snacks

94% fat-free microwave popcorn bags
    Jolly Time Healthy Pop, Orville Redenbacher's SmartPop!,
    Pop Secret 100 Calorie Pop

Crackers with fiber
    Melba Toast, Melba Snacks, Ryvita, Wasa

Reduced-fat baked and popped chips (preferably 100-calorie bags)
    Popchips, Quaker Popped Chips, Kettle Brand Bakes

Rice cakes and mini rice cakes
    Quaker

Freeze-dried fruit
    Funky Monkey, Just Tomatoes, Etc!

Snack Bars and Sweet Treats

Cereal bars, protein bars, and chewy granola bars with
    100 calories or less
    Quaker, Fiber One (especially Protein!), Special K

Quest Bars

Fiber One 90 Calorie Brownies and dessert bars

Vitalicious VitaTops (freezer aisle)

Nuts

Pistachios in the shell
Everybody's Nuts!, Wonderful Pistachios

Almonds (whole and sliced)
Blue Diamond 100-calorie packs,
Emerald 100-calorie packs, Wonderful Almonds,
Wonderful Almond Accents

BREAD

Light bread slices
Weight Watchers, Nature's Own 40 Calories, Nature's Own
Double Fiber, Arnold/Oroweat, Sara Lee 45 Calories &
Delightful, Pepperidge Farm Light Style, Pepperidge Farm
Very Thin, Fiber One

100-calorie flat sandwich buns
Flatout Foldits (Hungry Girl varieties and others!),
Arnold/Brownberry/Oroweat Sandwich Thins, Pepperidge
Farm Deli Flats, Nature's Own Sandwich Rounds,
Weight Watchers Flat Rolls, Sara Lee Thin Style Buns

Light English muffins
Thomas', Western Bagel Alternative, Weight Watchers,
Fiber One, Nature's Own 100 Calorie

What Are VitaTops?

They're all-natural, high-fiber, low-fat muffin tops with
just 100 calories (or less) each. REALLY satisfying and so
delicious! You can find the Deep Chocolate and a few
other flavors at select markets. You can also order online
at Vitalicious.com.

FROZEN DESSERTS

Low-fat fudge bars with 100 calories or less
   Weight Watchers Giant, Skinny Cow,
   Healthy Choice Premium, Fudgsicles

Enlightened The Good-For-You Ice Cream bars

Fruit bars with 100 calories or less
   Blue Bunny FrozFruit, Fruitfull Juice Bars,
   Dreyer's/Edy's Fruit Bars

SAUCES, SALAD DRESSINGS, AND SHELF-STABLE CONDIMENTS

Sauces and marinades with 20 calories or less per
      1-tablespoon serving
   Lawry's, Margie's, Ken's Steak House, Mrs. Dash,
   Newman's Own

Dressings with 20 calories or less per 1-tablespoon serving
   Newman's Own Lite (especially Low Fat Sesame Ginger),
   Ken's Light Options, Kraft Light, Wish-Bone Light

Vinegar (balsamic, rice, red wine, white wine, cider)

Light mayonnaise

Mustard (honey, Dijon, spicy brown, yellow)

PANTRY STAPLES, SPICES, AND MORE

No-calorie sweetener packets
   Splenda, Equal, Truvia, Stevia In The Raw, Nectresse

Salt-free seasoning mixes
   Mrs. Dash (Original Blend!), McCormick Perfect Pinch

Olive oil or grapeseed oil
   Pompeian

DINING OUT
ON THE PLAN

As you know, you'll get the best weight-loss results by preparing your own meals as often as possible. But dining out is a part of life, and there are plenty of smart choices you can make that fit into the plan. Here are diet-friendly meals for every dining-out occasion . . .

BREAKFAST

B.Y.O.N.: Bring Your Own Nuts! Keep a ½-ounce portion of almonds or pistachios (about 12 almonds or 24 pistachios) on you at all times. It's perfect for yogurt-based breakfasts or as a stand-alone emergency snack!

Diners, Restaurants, and Convenience Stores . . .

Fruit and Yogurt with Nuts

Pair 6 ounces (about ⅔ cup) of fat-free Greek yogurt with a large apple, banana, orange, or fresh fruit salad (about 1½ cups). If Greek isn't available, go with regular fat-free yogurt. Add ½ ounce of almonds or pistachios (about 12 almonds or 24 pistachios). Great option!

Egg-White or Egg Beaters Omelette

Order an omelette or scramble made with Egg Beaters or egg whites, veggies (tomato, peppers, and onions are best), and no cheese. Request very little (or no) oil/butter when your scramble is cooked. Get an English muffin (if available) or one piece of whole-wheat bread. Instead of butter, add a small amount (a teaspoon or so) of jam to the muffin or bread. Have a small fruit salad or piece of fruit on the side.

BREAKFAST

Fast Food . . .

Fruit and Yogurt Parfait

Skip the granola and honey, and stick with fresh fruit and yogurt, preferably light or fat-free. If there's a fat-free Greek option, even better! Add ½ ounce of almonds or pistachios (about 12 almonds or 24 pistachios). If the parfait is on the small side, order a side of fruit: apple slices are often available.

Egg-White English Muffin Sandwich

These are very popular and can be found at many restaurant chains. Skip the sausage and bacon, but feel free to have a single slice of cheese and naturally lean Canadian bacon. Pair with a small order of mixed fruit.

Fast-Food Bonus! Since nutritional stats are often provided, check 'em out before ordering. Your breakfast should have between 300 and 350 calories (200 to 250 before nuts, if adding).

About oatmeal . . . Although HG-style growing oatmeal is on the diet plan, I don't necessarily recommend getting oatmeal on the go. Why? Because ordinary oatmeal isn't all that satisfying. (Turn to the photo insert to see the size comparison!) However, if you can't find any of the above suggestions, oatmeal can be a decent choice. Go for a single serving made with water or fat-free milk. If the oatmeal's made with water, have a 6-ounce glass of fat-free milk on the side. A small topping of dried fruit is okay, but fresh fruit is better. If nutritionals are provided, look for options with 300 calories or less. And if hard-boiled eggs are available, have two whites on the side but skip the yolks.

LUNCHES AND DINNERS

Must-Know Info!
(View Before You Chew)

Before perusing the specific menu recommendations, get familiar with these easy guidelines . . .

Go-Anywhere Protein Preferences!
Order lean fish (like tilapia, cod, or sea bass), shrimp, or chicken, and have it baked, broiled, or grilled. Request that it be prepared dry or with very little oil, and then skip the sauce and opt for a squeeze of lemon. The serving size should be about 4 ounces. Think back to your Week 1 meals and what that serving size looks like. If the portion looks large, eyeball 4 ounces, and take the rest home for another meal.

Go-Anywhere Salad Advice!
Request no croutons, cheese, or crunchy toppings. You'll want to stick with salads made up of raw veggies: leafy greens, tomatoes, onions, peppers, etc. Ask for either oil and vinegar or low-fat/light dressing on the side. For a dinner salad, stick with a teaspoon or so of oil and a couple of tablespoons of vinegar, or have about 2 tablespoons of the dressing on the side. (Dip your fork in it, don't pour it over your salad.) For a side salad, top with vinegar and a drizzle of oil (about ½ teaspoon), or have a tablespoon of the dressing.

Go-Anywhere Hot-Veggie Advice!
Steamed veggies without butter or oil are your best bet. If steaming isn't an option, get your veggies grilled, but request little to no oil. For extra flavor, add a squeeze of lemon or a drizzle of balsamic vinegar.

When in Doubt, Calorie Count!
There are many diet-friendly meals on the pages that follow. Some require a little special ordering, but there's almost ALWAYS some version of these available. If you can't find something listed here and nutritional information is provided, look for meals with 300 to 350 calories. If you can only find something in the range of 400 to 450 calories, go for it; just skip one of your snacks that day.

LUNCHES AND DINNERS

Diners and American Restaurants . . .

Seafood or Chicken with Hot Veggies and Salad
You can get this meal almost anywhere. Follow the
go-anywhere advice on the previous page!

Salad with Grilled Chicken or Turkey Breast
Another easy-to-find staple. Don't be afraid to special order . . .
Just ask nicely!

Shrimp Cocktail with Dinner Salad
Enjoy the shrimp as your appetizer, or have it served with
your salad. (I like to put the shrimp on top of my salad!)

Fast Food . . .

Salad with Grilled Chicken
Those dressing packets often contain 2 ounces, about ¼ cup.
So stick with half, or request salsa instead!

Grilled Chicken Sandwich on a Lettuce Bun
Skip the cheese, bacon, and mayo, and go for mustard and/or
ketchup. If the place doesn't do "lettuce buns," simply ask for
extra lettuce in place of bread. Pair with a side salad!

LUNCHES AND DINNERS

Italian Food . . .

Seafood or Chicken with Hot Veggies and Salad
Remember to order your protein baked, broiled, or grilled. Add a little marinara to flavor up your protein *and* your veggies. Mmmmm!

Steamed Mussels or Clams with Marinara Sauce
Four ounces is the equivalent of about 14 large mussels or clams. Nice! Order a side salad and steamed veggies, and toss some marinara on those veggies.

Chinese Food . . .

Steamed Shrimp, Scallops, or Chicken with Veggies
These meals are often served with *twice* the amount of protein you need. Stick with about 4 ounces, and take the rest home to eat the next day. But enjoy all those veggies! And don't forget to skip the sauce. Dress your meal with a splash of soy sauce or a squeeze of lemon.

HG FYI: Those crispy noodles on the table are loaded with calories and fat. Avoid them at all costs!

LUNCHES AND DINNERS

Japanese Food . . .

Sashimi with Sunomono (Cucumber), Seaweed, or Green Salad
Ten pieces of sashimi (fish without rice) is the perfect amount—about 5 ounces of fish, in total. A little ginger, wasabi, and soy sauce seal the deal.

Chicken Teriyaki with Veggies, Hold the Teriyaki Sauce
See if they'll steam the meal for you. And add a splash of soy sauce for low-calorie flavor!

Mexican Food . . .

Salad with Grilled Chicken or Shrimp
In addition to the guidelines in the Go-Anywhere Salad Advice! section (page 101), skip the guacamole and sour cream. And whatever you do, avoid those giant fried tortilla shells! Salsa makes a great salad dressing at Mexican restaurants.

Chicken or Shrimp Fajitas
You *have* to be careful with this order. Request it prepared with as little oil as possible, and lots of veggies. Skip all the fatty extras, and stick with lettuce, pico de gallo, and black beans. Then load up two small corn tortillas until they overflow! Enjoy any remaining protein and veggies on the side.

LUNCHES AND DINNERS

Sandwich Shop . . .

Salad with Turkey Breast or Grilled Chicken

Pile on flavorful sandwich fixins, but skip the usual high-calorie suspects: cheese, mayo, bacon, etc. If the protein amount seems meager, request double!

Turkey Breast or Grilled Chicken over Shredded Lettuce

If salads aren't on the menu, order a small sub sans bun, and get your goodies over a bed of shredded lettuce.

Convenience-Store Emergency Meal!

If you find yourself on the go with no real lunch or dinner options in sight, assemble this diet-friendly hodgepodge . . . NICE!

* 4 hard-boiled egg whites

* 2 sticks of light string cheese (or 1 stick regular string cheese)

* 1 large apple or medium banana

* ¼ ounce of almonds or pistachios (about 6 almonds or 12 pistachios)

The Sodium Situation . . .

The meals and snacks in the book were carefully developed and/or chosen with sodium content in mind. That's one reason why not every food or product typically recommended by Hungry Girl fits into this particular diet plan.

If you need to be extra careful about your sodium intake, here are some tips & tricks to help . . .

Always choose unsalted nuts. I actually PREFER no-salt-added almonds and pistachios to salted versions. I think they taste better!

For salads, stick with oil and vinegar as opposed to dressing. The one exception? The Creamy Balsamic Dressing on page 196!

When it comes to sliced turkey, make *sure* you choose the no-salt-added kind. Reduced-sodium and even low-sodium options have more sodium than you might expect. If you don't see any prepackaged no-salt-added turkey, check the deli counter. The kind by Boar's Head is fantastic!

If buying precooked chicken, check the labels and look for ones with low sodium counts. Your best bet, however, is to cook it yourself with salt-free seasonings. Check out page 110 for how-to info!

If a meal calls for chicken *or* shrimp, choose chicken. It's naturally lower in sodium. And shrimp (even raw) often contains some added salt.

When choosing sauces, dressings, or marinades with 25 calories or less per 1-tablespoon serving (a staple ingredient in Week 1), select ones with the lowest sodium counts. Mrs. Dash has a lineup that's completely free of salt!

Swap premade salsa for diced tomatoes, onions, and herbs. Start with a can of no-salt-added diced tomatoes to save time!

When it comes to beans, rinsing them (as called for in the meals in the book) eliminates about 35 percent of the sodium amount listed on the can. Seek out no-salt-added beans to save even more.

Choose snacks with little to no sodium: fresh fruit (any kind), unsalted almonds or pistachios, veggies (your pick), freeze-dried fruit, certain rice cakes (check the labels), frozen fruit bars, and more. Flip to page 188 for the exact serving sizes.

This might go without saying, but when a meal calls for an occasional dash of salt, leave it out.

The suggested daily meal plans are designed to give you an easy guide to weight loss, but you can mix 'n match meals however you like. So browse around, and choose the meals with the lowest sodium counts!

HELPFUL HOW-TOS

How to Hard-Boil Egg Whites . . .

Place the eggs in a pot and cover completely with water, leaving a few inches of the pot's inner edge above the water line. Bring to a boil, and then continue to cook for 10 minutes. Drain the water, and fill the pot with very cold water. (Add ice if you've got it.) Once cool enough to handle, peel off the shells, slice in half, and remove the yolks.

How to Bake Spaghetti Squash . . .

Preheat oven to 400 degrees.

Microwave squash for 3 to 4 minutes, until soft enough to cut. Halve lengthwise; scoop out and discard seeds. Fill a large baking pan with ½ inch water, and place squash halves in the pan, cut sides down.

Bake until tender, about 40 minutes. (Check it at 30 minutes, if you like it on the firm side.)

Use a fork to scrape out squash strands. Place in a strainer to drain excess moisture. Blot dry, if needed!

How to Microwave Spaghetti Squash . . .

Microwave squash for 3 to 4 minutes, until soft enough to cut. Slice into quarters. Scoop out and discard seeds.

Place one piece of squash in a wide microwave-safe bowl, cut side down. Add 2 tablespoons water, cover, and cook for 8 minutes, or until soft. Repeat with remaining squash.

Use a fork to scrape out squash strands. Place in a strainer to drain excess moisture. Blot dry, if needed!

How to Cook Broccoli Cole Slaw or Chopped Cabbage in a Skillet . . .

Bring a large skillet sprayed with nonstick spray to medium-high heat. Add slaw or cabbage and ½ cup water. Cover and cook until fully softened, 10 to 12 minutes. Uncover and, if needed, cook and stir until water has evaporated, 2 to 3 minutes.

How to Steam Veggies in the Microwave . . .

For 1 to 3 cups of most veggies . . .

Place veggies in a microwave-safe bowl with 2 tablespoons water. Cover and microwave for 3 minutes, or until softened. Repeat as needed. Drain or blot dry.

How to Cook Chicken à la HG . . .

Place raw boneless skinless chicken breast on a baking sheet sprayed with nonstick spray, and sprinkle with some salt-free seasoning mix (like Mrs. Dash Original Blend). Bake at 375 degrees until cooked through, about 20 minutes. (Cook time will be longer for large batches.) Easy and delicious!

P.S. For perfectly cooked chicken, use a food thermometer, and bake until the internal temperature is 165 degrees.

Skillet Alternative! Pound chicken to 1/2-inch thickness. Bring a skillet sprayed with nonstick spray to medium heat. Cook chicken for about 5 minutes per side, until cooked through. Sprinkle with salt-free seasoning mix.

HG's High-Fiber Veggies

Tomatoes
Onions
Bell peppers
Green beans
Sugar snap peas
Snow peas
Bean sprouts
Broccoli
Brussels sprouts
Carrots
Jicama

HG's High-Volume Veggies

Mushrooms
Cucumbers
Cabbage
Celery
Zucchini
Eggplant
Yellow squash
Asparagus
Cauliflower
Kale
Spinach

HUNGRY GIRL'S GUIDE TO EXERCISE

While you absolutely CAN lose weight on this plan without any exercise at all, the truth is you'll drop weight faster if you work out . . . even a little bit. Burning extra calories means dropping extra pounds. The thought of exercising used to upset me. I couldn't get into it for the longest time . . . until I stopped trying to force myself into doing things that worked for *other* people and found ways to move that I LIKE. My go-to form of exercise is walking on the treadmill. I do this four to five times a week—for 45 minutes to an hour at a time—while watching my favorite TV shows on my DVR. This, plus weight/resistance training twice a week, works for me. I strongly recommend finding an exercise routine that YOU enjoy.

So let's talk calorie burning . . .

Find What Works for YOU

I told you about my routine, and now it's time for you to find yours. Making your workouts FUN is crucial. The trick might be working out while talking with a friend, listening to upbeat music while you lift free weights, swimming, dancing, speed-walking through the mall . . . Experiment! You might be surprised to find out that Hula-hooping or hiking does it for you.

Be Realistic

If you've never exercised before noon in your life, yet you've made up your mind to hit the 6 a.m. cycling class five times a week, you probably won't do it. So don't set yourself up for failure. Choose mini goals that you can *truly* see yourself achieving. Once you meet those, you'll have the confidence to take it to the next level.

Schedule Workouts

Setting exercise appointments can really help you to establish a routine. If they're written in your calendar, you'll be more likely to show up (as opposed to talking yourself out of them on lazy Sunday mornings). If you're still skipping out, try scheduling them with a friend. Or sign up for a class that takes place the same time each week. You can even plan to walk in place while watching your favorite nightly talk show. Try it!

Embrace Mini Workouts

It can be difficult to carve out an entire hour each day for a full-on fitness routine. But studies show that even short bouts of moderate to vigorous activity throughout the day are highly effective. So consider an exercise plan of 15-minute cardio sessions: one in the morning, one on your lunch break, and one before dinner. Feels much more achievable, doesn't it? You don't even need to do the same thing each time. Do a little dancing in your kitchen in the morning, power walk with a pal in the afternoon, and hop on the treadmill or go for a short jog after work. Go, you!

The Buddy System

The old saying that there's strength in numbers couldn't be more applicable than when talking about exercise. Not only is it fun to have company on the move-more bandwagon, but working out with friends means extra encouragement *and* accountability.

If you want to start simple, set lunch-break dates to go walking around the neighborhood or nearby mall. Then work up to activities like biking and jogging. Sign up for a group exercise class, or just go to the gym with a buddy. Even if you both do completely different activities at the gym, going together (or meeting up) will help get you there.

And if you've got a dog (or a rare leash-trained cat—okay, never mind), you've got a walking buddy! Take him or her to the park, and throw a Frisbee around. Any extra playtime is usually very much appreciated. Plus, your furry pal needs exercise to stay healthy, too!

An All-or-Nothing Attitude? So Last Season

Just like your new eating habits, if you slip up and miss a day of exercise, don't beat yourself up or use it as an excuse to scrap the whole thing. There will probably be days when you're busy and aren't able to get in much physical activity. That's life. Just get back to it the next day.

Every Bit Counts

Small activities DO add up—even if they don't feel like exercise—so commit to doing at least SOME extra physical activity each day. For example . . .

Clothes shopping. Seriously. Once I wore a calorie tracker to Nordstrom Rack and found that I burned more than 200 calories trying on clothes. (Yes, I tried on A LOT.)

Simple household chores—scrub and vacuum your way to smaller pants and a cleaner home! I'm all about multitasking . . .

Running errands? Do a few calf raises while waiting in line, park a little farther from your destination to get in some extra walking, and always take the stairs instead of the elevator.

Puttering around the house? Do bicep curls with soup cans while you wait for the oven to preheat. Stretch while you're waiting for your shower to heat up. Do jumping jacks during commercial breaks.

Once you start thinking about exercise like this, you'll find dozens of opportunities each day to sneak in some calorie burn!

The $5 Investment Every Exercise-Loathing Individual Should Make

If workouts *still* make you cringe, do yourself a favor and pick up a basic pedometer, a.k.a. step counter. Then simply aim to walk more throughout each day. Many experts say 10,000 steps is a great daily goal. But if you only hit 4,000 a day for the first few days you wear it, just keep setting mini improvement goals. Shoot for 5,500 steps during Week 1. Then aim for 7,000 in Week 2. By the end of the four-week plan, you'll be up to 10,000 per day. You have to start somewhere, and this is a great place to begin . . .

Budget-Friendly Fitness Ideas

Gym memberships, exercise classes, and fancy equipment can all get pricey. Luckily, there are plenty of cost-effective methods, no matter what type of activities you enjoy . . .

Chances are you own a workout DVD or two, and that you've gotten bored with them. Pool resources with your friends, and set up a swapping program, so each of you can try each other's workout DVDs without having to buy anything new. You can also find free videos online and at the local library. You might even be surprised to learn that your current cable provider has videos on demand. And there's more to the exercise-by-video craze than you might think. You can find instructor-led activities like yoga, martial arts, strength training, and more. They're a fantastic way to get the expertise and encouragement of a trainer without having to pay a fortune or brave a room full of strangers.

And you can't go wrong just cranking your favorite tunes, and getting your heart rate up. So go for a fast-paced walk with your headphones on. Do some lunges, jump rope, or just freeform dance. Let loose, and have fun!

HG Reminder . . .

If you have a vigorous exercise routine (like an hour or more of sweat-inducing daily workouts), you may need additional calories to fuel you. So consider adding one of the supplemental snacks found on page 220 on days you partake in heart-pounding, calorie-torching activities.

Obligatory disclaimer: I'm not a trainer or fitness professional. (You know this!) As with any exercise routine, you may want to consult a doctor first.

VEGETARIAN MEALS AND MEATLESS ALTERNATIVES

While this diet wasn't specially developed for vegetarians, people who don't eat meat can easily follow the four-week jump-start plan. This section provides everything you need to know on the subject.

VEGETARIAN MEALS

These breakfasts, lunches, and dinners can be enjoyed as often as you like. Mix 'n match with other meals made with the meatless alternatives on the next page . . .

Breakfast:

Lunches and Dinners:

MEATLESS ALTERNATIVES

Here are some swaps that can be used in MANY other meals on this plan. Specific picks were chosen based on taste and nutritional info . . .

If a meal calls for chicken . . .

Look for faux-chicken products with 140 calories or less per 4-ounce serving. These come refrigerated and frozen, as both patties and strips. Choose the ones with the most protein and the least amount of sodium. If a meal calls for raw chicken, use one ounce less of the ready-to-eat faux chicken; then heat (if needed) and add to the finished dish.

HG Picks:

* MorningStar Farms Grillers Chik'n Veggie Patties (use 1½ patties for every 4 ounces cooked chicken)

* Lightlife Smart Strips Chick'n (use 4 ounces for every 4 ounces cooked chicken)

* Beyond Meat Chicken-Free Strips (use 3 ounces for every 4 ounces cooked chicken)

If a meal calls for ground beef . . .

Frozen ground-beef-style soy crumbles are a great alternative to ground beef. Use 1 cup for every 4 to 5 ounces of raw beef. For the Big Burger recipe (page 160), replace the beef patty with a hamburger-style meatless patty that has less than 150 calories and 5 grams of fat or less—the more protein, the better.

HG Picks:

* MorningStar Farms Meal Starters Grillers Recipe Crumbles

* Boca Ground Crumbles (Note: These are higher in sodium.)

* Gardein The Ultimate Beefless Burger

MEATLESS ALTERNATIVES

NEED-TO-KNOW SODIUM INFO

Typically, meatless alternatives like these have significantly more sodium than meat, so the meals you use them in will have higher sodium counts. In order to offset the additional sodium, follow these tips . . .

* Since most of the breakfasts are vegetarian friendly, stick with the ones that have the lowest sodium counts. In general, the fruit and yogurt bowls are your best bets.

* Choose snacks with little to no sodium: fresh fruit (any kind), unsalted almonds or pistachios, veggies (your pick), freeze-dried fruit, certain rice cakes (check the labels), frozen fruit bars, and more. Flip to page 188 for the exact serving sizes. And don't forget about the Speedy Snacks and Snack Recipes, like the Berry-Citrus Slush (page 202), Apple Pie in a Mug (page 203), and Chocolate-Chip-Stuffed Strawberries (page 217)!

* If the meal you're making veggie friendly calls for any added salt, skip it. And when choosing meals, go with ones that have the lowest sodium counts to begin with.

* When having a salad that offers a dressing alternative, stick with the oil & vinegar or the low-sodium Creamy Balsamic Dressing.

WEEK 1 MEALS

You can (and should!) enjoy these meals throughout the entire plan.

BREAKFASTS

Mega Fruit 'n Yogurt Bowl

313 calories, 7.5g fat, 134mg sodium, 50g carbs, 13g fiber, 27g sugars, 22g protein

6 ounces (about ⅔ cup) fat-free plain Greek yogurt

1 no-calorie sweetener packet (optional)

⅛ teaspoon cinnamon, or more to taste

1½ cups chopped apple (about 1 medium apple) *or* 100 calories' worth of any fruit (see HG's Fruit Chart on page 192)

¼ cup Fiber One Original bran cereal*

½ ounce almonds or pistachios (about 12 almonds or 24 pistachios)

In a medium bowl, mix sweetener (optional) and cinnamon into yogurt. Top with fruit, cereal, and nuts!

> *Fiber One is sweetened with aspartame. If you prefer a high-fiber cereal made without artificial sweeteners, use All-Bran Original.

No-Calorie Sweetener Packets

Over the years, my attitude about these has changed a little. I used to consume more no-calorie sweetener than I currently do. I don't avoid sugar substitutes—and I still use them in my recipes—but I enjoy them in moderation. Choose the kind you like the best. Stevia and stevia-based sweeteners are all-natural and therefore a current favorite for many people.

Why Greek Yogurt?

I love yogurt—all kinds. But fat-free GREEK yogurt is especially great, because it's thick, creamy, and LOADED with protein. A few years ago, I was so convinced that fat-free Greek yogurt actually had fat that I took it to a lab to be tested. The results showed that it was completely fat-free! Very impressive—it's a staple in my life and on this plan.

BREAKFASTS

Egg Scramble & Bun

314 calories, 7g fat, 612mg sodium, 42g carbs, 14g fiber, 10g sugars, 26g protein

One 100-calorie flat sandwich bun or light English muffin
1 tablespoon light whipped butter or light buttery spread
¾ cup egg whites or fat-free liquid egg substitute
¼ cup chopped tomato *or* 2 large tomato slices

Optional seasonings: garlic powder, onion powder, black pepper

Side: 1 cup raspberries and/or blackberries*

Toast bun/muffin halves, if you like, and spread with butter. In a large microwave-safe mug sprayed with nonstick spray, microwave egg whites/substitute for 1 ½ minutes. Stir and microwave for 1 minute, or until set. Or just scramble in a skillet sprayed with nonstick spray. Top with chopped tomato or enjoy with tomato slices. Serve with berries.

> *Raspberries and blackberries are some of the most fiber-dense foods on the planet. Naturally occurring fiber is filling. Strawberries can be substituted, but fiber count will be lower.

Why Egg Substitute?

I'm a huge fan of eggs, but more often than not, I'm a yolk skipper. (You can call me by that nickname if you ever run into me!) Each yolk has around 55 calories and 5g fat, and those stats add up quickly. I enjoy fat-free liquid egg substitutes (like Egg Beaters Original), which are made mostly of egg whites. They're convenient and taste great. You can use either egg whites or egg substitute on this plan.

Egg Mug FYI: When choosing a mug, the bigger, the better. The egg rises as it cooks. Don't own any oversized mugs? Use a microwave-safe bowl.

WEEK 1 MEALS

BREAKFASTS

Growing Oatmeal B-fast

337 calories, 6.5g fat, 357mg sodium, 48.5g carbs, 9.5g fiber, 15g sugars, 22g protein

½ cup old-fashioned oats
1 no-calorie sweetener packet
¼ teaspoon cinnamon
Dash salt
¾ cup fat-free milk
⅛ teaspoon vanilla extract
¼ cup canned pure pumpkin
¼ cup raspberries and/or blackberries
¼ ounce almonds or pistachios (about 6 almonds *or* 12 pistachios)

Side: 2 large hard-boiled egg whites (how-to info on page 109)

In a nonstick pot, combine all oatmeal ingredients except pumpkin, berries, nuts, and eggs. Mix in 1¼ cups water. Bring to a boil and then reduce to a simmer. Add pumpkin and cook and stir until thick and creamy, 12 to 15 minutes. Transfer to a medium bowl and let slightly cool and thicken. Top with berries and nuts, or have 'em on the side with your egg whites!

> **HG Alternative:** Instead of hard-boiling the egg whites, scramble them up. A serving of two large egg whites is equal to ¼ cup egg whites or fat-free liquid egg substitute. In a microwave-safe mug sprayed with nonstick spray, microwave egg whites/substitute for 1 minute. Stir and microwave for 30 seconds, or until set. Or just scramble in a skillet sprayed with nonstick spray. Season with spices like garlic powder, onion powder, and black pepper.

> **Another HG Alternative:** Instead of egg whites, you can add ⅓ ounce (about 2 tablespoons) vanilla protein powder to your oatmeal bowl after cooking. Look for one with around about 100 calories per scoop, like Designer Whey.

BREAKFASTS

Why Raspberries and Blackberries?

Berries are a universally revered food. They're delicious, fun to eat, and REALLY good for you. You'll notice that I call out raspberries and blackberries a lot in this plan. Why? For a few reasons. They give you a huge bang for your calorie buck (a running theme in my life and in this book!) and are tremendously high in fiber. In fact, they're some of the most fiber-dense foods in the world—meaning they have more fiber per calorie than practically any other food. (COOL!) Fiber is essential—it helps you feel fuller longer and is typically lacking in the American diet. Do you need more reasons to love these berries as much as I do? Probably not, but in case you do, here's another. A 100-calorie serving of raspberries or blackberries is LARGE (about 1½ cups) and contains around 12 grams of fiber! Berries are nutritional superstars. Keep that in mind, now and forever.

Cook Your Growing Oatmeal in the Microwave!

Combine all ingredients *except* berries and nuts in a very large microwave-safe bowl (at least 10-cup capacity—your oatmeal will bubble up while it cooks!). Mix in 1¼ cups water. Microwave for 12 to 15 minutes, until thick and creamy, stirring halfway through. Let slightly cool and thicken.

Growing Oatmeal FYI: This oatmeal cooks for twice as long as standard oatmeal, and it WILL thicken up. Don't worry if it seems like a lot of liquid at the beginning. And old-fashioned slow-cooking oats are a must. Instant won't work in this recipe.

LUNCHES & DINNERS

Ginormous Salad with Chicken, Turkey, or Tuna

341 calories, 7.5g fat, 315mg sodium, 34g carbs, 11.5g fiber, 13.5g sugars, 38.5g protein

4 cups chopped romaine or iceberg lettuce

4 ounces cooked and chopped skinless chicken breast, no-salt-added turkey breast (about 8 slices), or low-sodium tuna packed in water (drained)

1 cup sugar snap peas, red bell pepper, carrots, and/or other high-fiber veggies (see HG's High-Fiber Veggies list on page 111)

1 cup cucumber, mushrooms, and/or other high-volume veggies (see HG's High-Volume Veggies list on page 111)

¼ cup canned black beans, garbanzo beans/chickpeas, or kidney beans, drained and rinsed

2 tablespoons vinegar (balsamic, red wine, white wine, rice, or cider)

1 teaspoon extra-virgin olive oil or grapeseed oil

In a large bowl, combine all ingredients except *vinegar and oil.*

Whisk vinegar with oil. Drizzle over salad, or serve it on the side!

> **HG Alternative:** Instead of vinegar, whisk the oil with 1 serving (3 to 4 tablespoons) Sweet 'n Tangy Tomato Dressing, Creamy Cilantro Dressing, or Creamy Balsamic Dressing (page 196). So good! Sodium count will vary.

> **Another HG Alternative:** Replace both the vinegar *and* the oil with 65 calories' worth of bottled dressing, preferably made with olive oil. Look for options with 150mg sodium or less.

LUNCHES & DINNERS

In a Hurry? Use a bagged salad mix of pre-chopped greens. Just make sure there are no nuts, tortilla strips, or other fancy extras.

Need chicken cooking tips? Check out page 110. If buying precooked chicken, choose options lower in sodium.

Why Olive Oil and Grapeseed Oil?

First, a word about healthy fats. It's classic, old-school diet mentality to think that fat is the enemy and we should avoid it. But that's just not the case. Monounsaturated and polyunsaturated fats—the kinds in olive and grapeseed oils as well as in almonds and pistachios—are extremely healthy. And studies show they can help keep you feeling fuller longer. So DON'T leave out the healthy fats on this plan . . . Learn to love them! Just measure carefully to keep the calories in check. (This is key.)

Most people know that olive oil is full of those good fats and consider it *the* go-to oil in the kitchen. Well, grapeseed oil is just as impressive (if not more!). Its mild flavor and high smoke point make it incredibly versatile—it tastes fantastic with everything from salads to stir-frys. It's also loaded with vitamin E and antioxidants. Give it a try!

* WEEK 1 *

LUNCHES & DINNERS

HG Dips 'n Dressings at a Glance!

Find the full recipes and stats (including big-batch instructions) on page 196!

Sweet 'n Tangy Tomato Dip/Dressing

3 tablespoons canned crushed tomatoes

1 teaspoon seasoned rice vinegar

1 teaspoon finely chopped basil

1/8 teaspoon garlic powder

Creamy Cilantro Dip/Dressing

3 tablespoons fat-free plain Greek yogurt

1 tablespoon water

1 teaspoon finely chopped cilantro

1/2 teaspoon lime juice

1/8 teaspoon each cumin, garlic powder, onion powder

Dash each salt and black pepper

Creamy Balsamic Dip/Dressing

2 tablespoons fat-free plain Greek yogurt

1 tablespoon balsamic vinegar

Half a no-calorie sweetener packet

HG Alternatives: Instead of dunking your Sandwich Platter veggies in an HG dip, you can use 30 calories' worth of bottled fat-free dressing or dip. You can also have your veggies steamed (how-to info on page 110) and tossed with a tablespoon of sauce, dressing, or marinade with 30 calories or less. Sodium will vary.

LUNCHES & DINNERS

Super-Sized Sandwich Platter
with Tuna, Turkey, or Chicken

349 calories, 5.5g fat, 573mg sodium, 39g carbs, 10.5g fiber, 11g sugars, 40.5g protein

Sandwich

4 ounces low-sodium tuna packed in water (drained),
   no-salt-added turkey breast (about 8 slices), or cooked
   skinless chicken breast
2 teaspoons light mayonnaise
One 100-calorie flat sandwich bun *or* 2 slices light bread,
   toasted (optional)
1 large tomato slice
1 lettuce leaf

Optional seasonings: garlic powder, onion powder,
   Italian seasoning

Veggies and Dip

1½ cups sugar snap peas, red bell pepper, carrots,
   and/or other high-fiber veggies (page 111)
1 serving (3 to 4 tablespoons) Sweet 'n Tangy Tomato Dip,
   Creamy Cilantro Dip, or Creamy Balsamic Dip (page 196)

If having the tuna, mix it with mayo and optional ingredients. If you're packing your lunch to go, keep the tuna mixture separate from the bread until lunchtime.

To prepare the chicken, pound a 5-ounce raw boneless skinless chicken breast cutlet to ½-inch thickness. Bring a skillet sprayed with nonstick spray to medium heat. Cook for about 5 minutes per side, until cooked through. Season to taste with salt-free seasoning.

Assemble sandwich and enjoy with veggies and dip.

> **HG FYI:** If you don't see any prepackaged no-salt-added turkey, check the deli counter. I'm a big fan of Boar's Head deli meats. You can also cook up your own skinless turkey breast with salt-free seasonings. (It'll take about 5 ounces raw turkey to yield 4 ounces cooked.) Or just get the turkey with the lowest sodium count you can find.

LUNCHES & DINNERS

Veggie 'n Bean Bowl with Side of Greek Yogurt

333 calories, 6.5g fat, 683mg sodium, 38g carbs, 9.5g fiber, 13.5g sugars, 33g protein

1 ½ cups mushrooms, zucchini, and/or cauliflower

1 ½ cups shredded lettuce

½ cup canned black beans, garbanzo beans/chickpeas, or kidney beans, drained and rinsed

2 teaspoons vinegar (balsamic, red wine, white wine, rice, or cider)

¼ cup crumbled reduced-fat feta cheese

Side: 6 ounces (about ⅔ cup) fat-free Greek yogurt with 1 optional no-calorie sweetener packet

Place veggies in a microwave-safe bowl with 2 tablespoons water. Cover and microwave for 3 minutes, or until softened. Drain and blot dry. Alternatively, in a skillet sprayed with nonstick spray, cook and stir over medium-high heat until softened, about 5 minutes.

In a bowl, layer lettuce, beans, and veggies. Drizzle with vinegar, and sprinkle with cheese. Serve yogurt on the side (add sweetener, if you like).

> **HG FYI:** This meal is also great chilled!

LUNCHES & DINNERS

Mix 'n Match Mania! HG-ified Fish or Chicken with Hot Veggies and Salad

I love sauces, dressings, and marinades. My favorites are made by Margie's (obscure, but worth finding!), Lawry's (a supermarket staple), and Newman's Own (Lite Low Fat Sesame Ginger Dressing!). And by mixing and matching them with various proteins and veggies, there are countless ways to enjoy the HG-ified Fish or Chicken with Hot Veggies and Salad on the next page. Here are just a few ideas to get you started . . .

BBQ chicken with cabbage

Citrus cod with broccoli cole slaw

Lemon pepper tilapia with spaghetti squash

Herb & garlic cod with cabbage

Caribbean chicken with spaghetti squash

Southwestern tilapia with broccoli cole slaw

Balsamic sea bass with spaghetti squash

Chipotle chicken with cabbage

Zesty Italian cod with spaghetti squash

Sesame-ginger tilapia with cabbage

Chile-lime sea bass with spaghetti squash

Raspberry vinaigrette tilapia with broccoli cole slaw

Ranch chicken with spaghetti squash

LUNCHES & DINNERS

HG-ified Fish or Chicken with Hot Veggies and Salad

335 calories, 10g fat, 402mg sodium, 26g carbs, 8g fiber, 13.5g sugars, 35g protein

Fish or Chicken

5 ounces raw tilapia, cod, sea bass, or boneless skinless chicken breast

1 teaspoon salt-free seasoning mix (like Mrs. Dash Original Blend)

1 teaspoon sauce, dressing, or marinade with 25 calories or less per 1-tablespoon serving (like the ones by Lawry's)

Hot Veggies

3 cups chopped cabbage, 1½ cups cooked spaghetti squash strands (measured once cooked; how-to info on page 109), *or* 2½ cups bagged broccoli cole slaw

2 teaspoons sauce, dressing, or marinade with 25 calories or less per 1-tablespoon serving (like the ones by Lawry's)

1 teaspoon extra-virgin olive oil or grapeseed oil

Salad

1 cup lettuce

½ cup tomato, onion, and/or other high-fiber veggies (page 111)

½ cup cucumber, mushrooms, and/or other high-volume veggies (page 111)

2½ teaspoons vinegar (balsamic, red wine, white wine, rice, or cider)

½ teaspoon extra-virgin olive oil or grapeseed oil

Preheat oven to 350 degrees for fish or 375 degrees for chicken. Season fish or chicken with seasoning mix. Bake in a baking pan sprayed with nonstick spray until cooked through, 15 to 20 minutes. (If your fish fillet is on the thin side, check it at 10 minutes.) Drizzle with sauce, dressing, or marinade.

Steam cabbage/broccoli slaw or cook in a skillet (how-to info on page 110). Drizzle veggies with sauce, dressing, or marinade. Assemble salad and serve!

LUNCHES & DINNERS

Veggie FYI: Why cabbage, slaw, or squash? HUGE serving sizes! They're also loaded with fiber and really satisfying. You can also choose 1 ½ cups broccoli, cauliflower, Brussels sprouts, carrots, and/or asparagus.

Skillet Alternative! For chicken, pound to ½-inch thickness. Bring a skillet sprayed with nonstick spray to medium heat. Cook chicken or fish for 3 to 5 minutes per side, until cooked through. Sprinkle with salt-free seasoning mix.

For best results . . .
Use a food thermometer. Bake chicken until the internal temperature is 165 degrees; fish should be baked until 145 degrees.

Why Salt-Free Seasoning?

We all know it's important to keep sodium intake to a minimum. But I have a confession to make: I used to salt things—a LOT. And I didn't give salt-free seasonings the time of day. One day, I decided to experiment a little with them, and now I'm officially OBSESSED. These mixes can take a bland piece of chicken or fish and make it taste off-the-charts amazing. My hands-down favorite is Mrs. Dash Original Blend. It goes with everything! But I also recommend having a little fun with the dozens of flavors on shelves—citrus, chipotle, sweet 'n smoky . . . Both Mrs. Dash and McCormick make these.

Don't miss . . . The mix 'n match meal ideas on page 133!

LUNCHES & DINNERS

Chicken Hungry Girlfredo Bowl

340 calories, 8.5g fat, 693mg sodium, 24.5g carbs, 10.5g fiber, 10g sugars, 41g protein

This big fettuccine Alfredo swap can be made with tofu shirataki noodles OR broccoli cole slaw!

. . . with tofu shirataki noodles

1 bag House Foods Tofu Shirataki Fettuccine Shaped Noodle Substitute

2 tablespoons light sour cream

2 wedges The Laughing Cow Light Creamy Swiss cheese

4 ounces cooked skinless chicken breast, chopped or sliced

1½ cups steamed broccoli, cauliflower, Brussels sprouts, carrots, and/or asparagus (veggie-steaming info on page 110)

Optional seasonings: garlic powder, paprika

Use a strainer to rinse and drain noodles. Thoroughly pat dry. Roughly cut noodles. Bring a skillet sprayed with nonstick spray to medium heat. Add all ingredients except chicken and veggies, breaking the cheese wedges into pieces. Cook and stir until cheese has melted, mixed with sour cream, and coated noodles, 2 to 3 minutes. Top with chicken and steamed veggies (or serve veggies on the side).

. . . with broccoli cole slaw

One 12-ounce bag (4 cups) broccoli cole slaw

2 tablespoons light sour cream

2 wedges The Laughing Cow Light Creamy Swiss cheese

4 ounces cooked skinless chicken breast, chopped or sliced

Optional seasonings: garlic powder, paprika

Bring a large skillet sprayed with nonstick spray to medium-high heat. Add broccoli slaw and ½ cup water. Cover and cook until fully softened, 10 to 12 minutes. Uncover and, if needed, cook and stir until water has evaporated, 2 to 3 minutes. Add all other ingredients except chicken, breaking the cheese wedges into pieces. Cook and stir until cheese has melted, mixed with sour cream, and coated slaw, 2 to 3 minutes. Top with chicken.

LUNCHES & DINNERS

Why Tofu Shirataki Noodles?

I'm a huge fan of tofu shirataki noodles. Made of a combination of tofu and yam flour, they are an EXCELLENT pasta swap with a tiny fraction of the calories and carbs. They also have a nice amount of fiber and are all-natural, gluten-free, and very filling. These are different from the similar shirataki noodles that are made *without* any tofu. I find the addition of tofu not only makes these a little bit more filling, but it also gives them more of a pasta-like texture. I highly recommend trying them out in these noodle bowls and eating them frequently throughout the four weeks of this plan. Find them in the refrigerated section of the supermarket with the traditional tofu.

The Hungry Girlfredo Bowl is a go-to staple of mine for both lunch AND dinner, and I eat it several times a week . . . YUM!

Need help cooking up that chicken? Check out page 110. You can also find precooked chicken breast at the supermarket. Choose kinds lower in sodium.

HG Alternative: Steam your slaw by microwaving it right in the bag, if the package says it can be done. Then transfer to a microwave-safe bowl. Add all other ingredients *except* chicken, breaking the cheese wedges into pieces. Microwave for 3 minutes, and stir well. Top with chicken.

LUNCHES & DINNERS

HG's Special Stir-Fry

351 calories, 8.5g fat, 624mg sodium, 28.5g carbs, 7g fiber, 13.5g sugars, 38.5g protein

1 ½ cups small broccoli florets

1 ½ cups sliced bell pepper

½ cup sliced onion

1 teaspoon olive oil or grapeseed oil

5 ounces raw boneless skinless chicken breast, cut into bite-sized pieces

¼ teaspoon salt-free seasoning (like the ones by Mrs. Dash)

2 tablespoons sauce, dressing, or marinade with 25 calories or less per 1-tablespoon serving (like the ones by Lawry's)

Bring a large skillet sprayed with nonstick spray to medium-high heat. Add veggies, and drizzle with oil. Cook and stir until slightly softened, about 4 minutes. Add chicken, and sprinkle with seasoning. Cook and stir until veggies are soft and chicken is cooked through, about 4 more minutes. Add sauce, dressing, or marinade, and stir well.

> **Time-Saving Alternative:** Use 1 ½ cups frozen broccoli florets and 2 cups frozen stir-fry veggies!

> **Another Time-Saving Alternative:** Use 4 ounces precooked chicken breast, and add with the sauce, dressing, or marinade!

WEEK 1 MEALS

MEALS FOR WEEKS 2 - 4

BREAKFASTS

Growing Oatmeal FYI:

HG oatmeal cooks for twice as long as standard oatmeal, and it WILL thicken up. Don't worry if it seems like a lot of liquid at the beginning. And old-fashioned slow-cooking oats are a must. Instant won't work in these recipes.

Cook Your Growing Oatmeal in the Microwave!

You can use this method for all the oatmeal recipes except the parfait . . .

Instead of combining the specified ingredients in a nonstick pot, combine them in a very large microwave-safe bowl (at least 10-cup capacity—your oatmeal will bubble up while it cooks!). Mix in 1¼ cups water. Microwave for 12 to 15 minutes, until thick and creamy, stirring halfway through. Continue with recipe as directed.

DAY AT A GLANCE

94% Fat-Free
Microwave
Popcorn

Chocolate-Chip-Stuffed
Strawberries

li Rolls

The HG
Chop Chop

Chicken Hungry
Girlfredo Bowl

Veggie-Packed
Egg Mug B-fast

SUPER-SIZED SERVINGS

Just LOOK how much more food you get . . .

Traditional Oatmeal Breakfast
355 calories, 7g fat

HG's Growing Oatmeal B-fast
337 calories, 6.5g fat

Traditional Fettuccine Alfredo with Chicken
350 calories, 14g fat

HG's Chicken Hungry Girlfredo Bowl
340 calories, 8.5g fat

Traditional Chicken Caesar Salad
340 calories, 28g fat

HG's BBQ Chicken Salad
338 calories, 7g fat

Dried Apricots
100 calories, 0g fat

Fresh Watermelon
100 calories, 0g fat

Traditional Chicken Fingers
355 calories, 18.5g fat

HG's Faux-Fried Chicken Strips with Side Salad
347 calories, 8g fat

Traditional Yogurt and Granola
310 calories, 8.5g fat

HG's Tropical Fruit 'n Yogurt Bowl
307 calories, 7g fat

DINING OUT/ON THE GO

Find the Dining Out on the Plan section on page 98!

Egg-White Scramble with Toast and Fruit Salad

Greek Yogurt, Nuts, and Fruit

Sandwich-Shop Turkey Salad

Fast-Food Grilled Chicken Salad

Grilled Fish with Salad and Steamed Veggies

Steamed Shrimp and Mixed Veggies

SNACKS, SNACKS, SNACKS

Find these snacks and more beginning on page 184!

Snack-tastic Butternut Fries

CRAVING-BUSTERS!

Perfect Pizza-bella

Cheesy Faux-tato Skins

100-calorie bag of popped chips

Magical Margarita Light

Lord of the Onion Strings

DESSERT FIXES!

Caramel Apple Crunchcake

Low-fat frozen fudge bar

Vitalicious VitaTop

HUGE PORTIONS!

2 cups halved strawberries

2½ cups sliced bell peppers with ¼ cup fresh salsa

1½ cups spaghetti squash with ¼ cup low-fat marinara sauce

3⅓ cups sugar snap peas

Turkey breast with cucumber spears

Souper-Sized Soup

CRAVING-BUSTING MEALS

Knife & Fork Avocado Chicken B-fast Burrito

Chicken Parm with Saucy Pasta Swap

Big Burger with Side Salad

Chicken Fajita Tostadas

Chicken So Low Mein with Side Salad

Crunchy Beef Tacos with Side Salad

BREAKFASTS

Pumped-Up Protein Oatmeal

337 calories, 7g fat, 340mg sodium, 49.5g carbs, 9g fiber, 15g sugars, 20g protein

½ cup old-fashioned oats
2 no-calorie sweetener packets
⅛ teaspoon pumpkin pie spice
⅛ teaspoon cinnamon
Dash salt
¾ cup fat-free milk
½ cup canned pure pumpkin
⅓ ounce (about 2 tablespoons) vanilla protein powder with about 100 calories per full scoop
2 teaspoons light whipped butter or light buttery spread

In a nonstick pot, combine all ingredients except *pumpkin, protein powder, and butter. Mix in 1 ¼ cups water. Bring to a boil and then reduce to a simmer.*

Add pumpkin and cook and stir until thick and creamy, 12 to 15 minutes.

Transfer to a medium bowl, and stir in protein powder and butter. Let slightly cool and thicken.

Protein Powder Picks: Designer Whey and Rainbow Light

> **HG Alternative:** Not into protein powder? Have 2 large hard-boiled egg whites on the side instead.

BREAKFASTS

Strawberry Peach Oatmeal Parfait

344 calories, 8g fat, 361mg sodium, 50.5g carbs, 7.5g fiber, 25g sugars, 21g protein

Oatmeal

⅓ cup old-fashioned oats
1 no-calorie sweetener packet
¼ teaspoon cinnamon
⅛ teaspoon vanilla extract
Dash salt
¾ cup fat-free milk

Parfait

⅔ cup chopped peaches
⅔ cup chopped strawberries
⅓ ounce (about 1 ½ tablespoons) sliced almonds

Side: 2 large hard-boiled egg whites

Combine all oatmeal ingredients in a small nonstick pot. Mix in ¼ cup water.

Bring to a boil and then reduce to a simmer. Cook and stir until thick and creamy, 4 to 5 minutes.

Transfer to a medium bowl and let slightly cool. Cover and refrigerate until chilled, at least 1 ½ hours.

Stir oatmeal. In a tall glass, layer half of each ingredient: oatmeal, peaches, and strawberries.

Repeat layering with remaining oatmeal, peaches, and strawberries. Top with almonds, and serve with egg whites.

> **Time-Saving Tip:** Cook your oatmeal the night before, and let it chill overnight. In the morning, just assemble and eat!

BREAKFASTS

Apple Walnut Oatmeal

345 calories, 8g fat, 363mg sodium, 48g carbs, 8g fiber, 16g sugars, 21.5g protein

½ cup old-fashioned oats
¼ cup chopped apple
1 no-calorie sweetener packet
¼ teaspoon cinnamon
⅛ teaspoon vanilla extract
Dash salt
¾ cup fat-free milk
¼ cup canned pure pumpkin
¼ ounce (about 1 ½ teaspoons) chopped walnuts

Side: 2 large hard-boiled egg whites

In a nonstick pot, combine all ingredients except pumpkin, walnuts, and egg whites. Mix in 1 ¼ cups water. Bring to a boil and then reduce to a simmer. Add pumpkin and cook and stir until thick and creamy, 12 to 15 minutes.

Transfer to a medium bowl and let slightly cool and thicken. Top with nuts, and serve with egg whites!

The Hard-Boiled Truth: Tips & Alternatives

* To save time, prep a dozen hard-boiled egg whites at once. For a mini tutorial, flip to page 109.

* Whip up a mini scramble instead. Two large egg whites equals ¼ cup liquid egg whites/fat-free liquid egg substitute. In a microwave-safe mug sprayed with nonstick spray, microwave for 1 minute. Stir and microwave for 30 seconds, or until set. Or make your scramble in a skillet sprayed with nonstick spray.

* Don't like eggs? Just add ⅓ ounce (about 2 tablespoons) vanilla protein powder to your oatmeal after cooking it. Look for one with around 100 calories per scoop, like Designer Whey.

BREAKFASTS

Blueberry Almond Oatmeal

345 calories, 7g fat, 371mg sodium, 49.5g carbs, 8.5g fiber, 17g sugars, 22g protein

½ cup old-fashioned oats
1 no-calorie sweetener packet
¼ teaspoon cinnamon
⅛ teaspoon vanilla extract
Dash salt
¾ cup fat-free milk
¼ cup canned pure pumpkin
¼ cup blueberries
¼ ounce (about 1 tablespoon) sliced almonds

Side: 2 large hard-boiled egg whites

In a nonstick pot, combine all ingredients except *pumpkin, blueberries, almonds, and egg whites. Mix in 1¼ cups water. Bring to a boil and then reduce to a simmer. Add pumpkin and cook and stir until thick and creamy, 12 to 15 minutes.*

Transfer to a medium bowl and let slightly cool and thicken. Top with berries and nuts, and serve with egg whites!

> **HG FYI:** There's helpful oatmeal info on page 142 and tips about egg whites on page 145.

BREAKFASTS

Knife & Fork Avocado Chicken B-fast Burrito

335 calories, 7.5g fat, 650mg sodium, 46.5g carbs, 15.5g fiber, 10g sugars, 30g protein

1 medium-large high-fiber tortilla with 110 calories or less
2 cups chopped spinach leaves
¼ cup chopped onion
½ cup egg whites or fat-free liquid egg substitute
⅛ teaspoon each onion powder and garlic powder
Dash black pepper
1 ounce cooked and finely chopped skinless chicken breast
¼ cup seeded and diced tomato
1 ounce (about 2 tablespoons) diced avocado

Side: ⅔ cup raspberries and/or blackberries

Optional seasonings: chili powder and additional
onion powder, garlic powder, and black pepper

Microwave tortilla on a microwave-safe plate for 10 seconds, or until warm.

In a large microwave-safe mug, microwave spinach and onion for 2 minutes, or until softened. Blot away excess moisture, and distribute cooked veggies across the middle of the tortilla.

Spray the mug with nonstick spray, and add egg whites or substitute and spices. Microwave for 1 minute.

Stir in chicken. Microwave for 1 minute, or until set.

Distribute egg scramble over the cooked veggies, and top with tomato and avocado.

Wrap up tortilla by first folding one side in (to keep filling from escaping), and then rolling it up from the bottom.

Serve with fruit and devour!

HG Alternative: Skip the tortilla, and serve burrito contents with a 100-calorie flat sandwich bun or light English muffin.

BREAKFASTS

EggaMuffin B-fast

313 calories, 8.5g fat, 627mg sodium, 41.5g carbs, 14g fiber, 9.5g sugars, 24g protein

Sandwich

One 100-calorie flat sandwich bun or light English muffin
½ tablespoon light whipped butter or light buttery spread
1 slice Sargento reduced-fat cheddar cheese
⅓ cup egg whites or fat-free liquid egg substitute
Dash each garlic powder, onion powder, and black pepper
½ ounce (about 1 slice) reduced-sodium ham

Sides

2 large tomato slices
1 cup raspberries and/or blackberries

Toast bun or muffin halves, if you like, and spread with butter. Place cheese on the bottom half.

In a microwave-safe medium bowl or wide mug sprayed with nonstick spray, combine egg whites or substitute with spices. Microwave for 1 minute. Gently stir and microwave for 30 seconds, or until set.

Transfer egg "patty" to the cheese-topped half of the bun or muffin. Top with ham and the other bun or muffin half. If you like, microwave for 15 seconds, or until cheese has melted.

Serve with tomato slices and berries.

> **HG FYI:** This recipe calls for Sargento cheese because of its impressively low sodium count. If you can't find Sargento, get the reduced-fat cheddar cheese with the lowest sodium count.

Leftover Ham Tip: As one of your snacks, pair an ounce (about 2 slices) of reduced-sodium ham with 60 calories' worth of veggies (see 60-Calorie Veggie Portions on page 194)!

BREAKFASTS

Veggie-Packed Egg Mug B-fast

328 calories, 7.5g fat, 648mg sodium, 41.5g carbs, 11.5g fiber, 10g sugars, 29g protein

One 100-calorie flat sandwich bun or light English muffin
2 teaspoons light whipped butter or light buttery spread
½ cup sliced mushrooms
¼ cup chopped onion
¼ cup chopped asparagus
⅔ cup egg whites or fat-free liquid egg substitute
⅛ teaspoon each onion powder and garlic powder
Dash black pepper
2 tablespoons shredded reduced-fat cheddar or
    Mexican-blend cheese
¼ cup seeded and diced tomato

Side: ½ cup raspberries and/or blackberries

Toast bun or muffin halves, if you like, and spread with butter.

Spray a large microwave-safe mug with nonstick spray. Add mushrooms, onion, and asparagus. Microwave for 2 minutes, or until softened.

Blot away excess moisture. Add egg whites or substitute and spices, stir, and microwave for 1½ minutes.

Stir in cheese and tomato. Microwave for 1 minute, or until set. Serve with berries and buttered bun or muffin.

> **Egg Mug FYI:** When choosing a mug, the bigger, the better. The egg rises as it cooks. Don't own any oversized mugs? Use a microwave-safe bowl.

BREAKFASTS

The Great Greek Egg Breakfast

337 calories, 8g fat, 687mg sodium, 46g carbs, 14.5g fiber, 11g sugars, 26g protein

One 100-calorie flat sandwich bun or light English muffin
1 tablespoon light whipped butter or light buttery spread
½ cup chopped spinach leaves
¼ cup chopped red onion
⅔ cup egg whites or fat-free liquid egg substitute
2 tablespoons seeded and diced tomato
1 tablespoon crumbled reduced-fat feta cheese
½ tablespoon chopped fresh basil
⅛ teaspoon dried oregano

Side: 1 cup raspberries and/or blackberries

Toast bun or muffin halves, if you like, and spread with butter.

In a large microwave-safe mug sprayed with nonstick spray, microwave spinach and onion for 1 ½ minutes, or until softened.

Blot away excess moisture. Add egg whites or substitute, stir, and microwave for 1 ½ minutes.

Stir in remaining ingredients except berries. Microwave for 1 minute, or until set. Enjoy with berries and buttered bun or muffin.

> **Skillet Alternative!** Feel free to make your egg breakfast in a skillet sprayed with nonstick spray as opposed to a mug in the microwave.

BREAKFASTS

Tropical Fruit 'n Yogurt Bowl

307 calories, 7g fat, 160mg sodium, 48g carbs, 11.5g fiber, 28g sugars, 20.5g protein

6 ounces (about ⅔ cup) fat-free plain Greek yogurt
1 no-calorie sweetener packet
Dash cinnamon
½ cup sliced strawberries
½ cup pineapple chunks packed in juice, drained
¼ cup Fiber One Original bran cereal
¼ ounce (about 1 tablespoon) chopped pecans or sliced almonds
1 tablespoon sweetened shredded coconut

In a medium bowl, mix sweetener and cinnamon into yogurt. Top with remaining ingredients.

> **Fiber One 101:** Fiber One is sweetened with aspartame. If you prefer a high-fiber cereal made without artificial sweeteners, use All-Bran Original.

BREAKFASTS

Berry Madness Yogurt Bowl

321 calories, 8.5g fat, 141mg sodium, 48.5g carbs, 18.5g fiber, 21g sugars, 24g protein

6 ounces (about ⅔ cup) fat-free plain Greek yogurt
1 no-calorie sweetener packet
Dash cinnamon
1 cup raspberries and/or blackberries
½ cup blueberries
¼ cup Fiber One Original bran cereal
½ ounce (about 2 tablespoons) sliced almonds

In a medium bowl, mix sweetener and cinnamon into yogurt. Top with remaining ingredients.

BREAKFASTS

Banana-Berry Yogurt Bowl

322 calories, 8.5g fat, 125mg sodium, 50g carbs, 13g fiber, 22.5g sugars, 23g protein

6 ounces (about ⅔ cup) fat-free plain Greek yogurt
1 no-calorie sweetener packet
Dash cinnamon
¾ cup chopped strawberries
½ cup sliced banana
¼ cup Fiber One Original bran cereal
½ ounce (about 2 tablespoons) sliced almonds

*In a medium bowl, mix sweetener and cinnamon into yogurt.
Top with remaining ingredients.*

Download The
Hungry Girl Diet App
to create custom
shopping lists and track
your food! Visit
hungry-girl.com/diet
for details.

LUNCHES & DINNERS

MEALS FOR WEEKS 2 – 4

Chinese Chicken Salad

330 calories, 8g fat, 611mg sodium, 35g carbs, 11.5g fiber, 16g sugars, 35.5g protein

4 cups chopped romaine or iceberg lettuce

2 cups bagged cole slaw mix

4 ounces cooked and chopped skinless chicken breast

¼ cup mandarin orange segments packed in juice, drained

¼ cup canned sliced water chestnuts, roughly chopped

2 tablespoons Fiber One Original bran cereal

2 tablespoons chopped scallions

¼ ounce (about 1 tablespoon) sliced almonds

2 tablespoons low-fat sesame ginger dressing

Place all ingredients except *dressing in a large bowl. Drizzle dressing over salad, or serve it on the side!*

Need help cooking up that chicken? Check out page 110. You can also find precooked chicken breast at the supermarket. Choose ones lower in sodium.

LUNCHES & DINNERS

BBQ Chicken Salad

338 calories, 7g fat, 705mg sodium, 33g carbs, 11g fiber, 10.5g sugars, 38g protein

Dressing

1 tablespoon BBQ sauce with about 45 calories per 2-tablespoon serving
1 tablespoon fat-free plain Greek yogurt
¾ teaspoon ranch dressing/dip seasoning mix

Salad

4 cups chopped romaine or iceberg lettuce
4 ounces cooked and chopped skinless chicken breast
¼ cup chopped tomato
¼ cup peeled and chopped jicama

¼ cup canned black beans, drained and rinsed

1 ounce (about 2 tablespoons) chopped avocado
2 tablespoons frozen sweet corn kernels, thawed
1 tablespoon chopped cilantro

To make the dressing, in a small bowl, combine BBQ sauce, Greek yogurt, and ranch seasoning. Add 2 teaspoons water, and stir until uniform.

Place all salad ingredients in a large bowl. Top salad with dressing, or serve dressing on the side. Yum!

MEALS FOR WEEKS 2 – 4

LUNCHES & DINNERS

Veggie-rific Salad

337 calories, 9.5g fat, 630mg sodium, 38g carbs, 10.5g fiber, 14.5g sugars, 29.5g protein

4 cups chopped spinach leaves

1 cup sliced mushrooms

1 cup chopped cucumber

½ cup chopped bell pepper

½ cup chopped tomato

⅓ cup garbanzo beans/chickpeas, drained and rinsed

4 large hard-boiled egg whites, chopped

2 tablespoons crumbled reduced-fat feta cheese

2 tablespoons vinegar (balsamic, red wine, white wine, rice, or cider)

1 teaspoon extra-virgin olive oil or grapeseed oil

In a large bowl, combine all ingredients except vinegar and oil.

Whisk vinegar with oil. Drizzle over salad, or serve it on the side!

> **HG Alternative:** Instead of vinegar, use 1 serving (3 to 4 tablespoons) Sweet 'n Tangy Tomato Dressing, Creamy Cilantro Dressing, or Creamy Balsamic Dressing (page 196). Love these! Sodium count will vary.

LUNCHES & DINNERS

Fajita Salad

320 calories, 9.5g fat, 613mg sodium, 28.5g carbs, 7.5g fiber, 13.5g sugars, 32.5g protein

1 cup sliced onion
1 cup sliced red and green bell peppers
1 teaspoon olive oil or grapeseed oil
4 ounces cooked and chopped skinless chicken breast or ready-to-eat shrimp
1 teaspoon fajita seasoning
4 cups chopped romaine or iceberg lettuce
2 tablespoons salsa
2 tablespoons light sour cream

Bring a skillet sprayed with nonstick spray to medium heat. Add onion and peppers, and drizzle with oil. Cook and stir until softened and lightly browned, 8 to 10 minutes.

Add chicken or shrimp to the skillet, and sprinkle with fajita seasoning. Add 2 tablespoons water. Cook and stir until chicken or shrimp is hot and liquid has thickened, about 1 minute.

Let cool slightly, about 5 minutes.

Place lettuce in a large bowl. Top with chicken/shrimp–veggie mixture, salsa, and sour cream.

LUNCHES & DINNERS

Classic Chef Salad

324 calories, 10g fat, 554mg sodium, 27.5g carbs, 8.5g fiber, 13.5g sugars, 37g protein

4 cups chopped romaine or iceberg lettuce

1 plum tomato, cut into wedges

1 cup sliced cucumber

1 cup sliced mushrooms

1 cup bagged broccoli cole slaw

3 ounces (about 6 slices) no-salt-added turkey breast, chopped

1 hard-boiled egg white, cut into wedges

2 tablespoons shredded reduced-fat cheddar or Mexican-blend cheese

2 tablespoons light Thousand Island or French dressing

Optional seasoning: black pepper

Place all ingredients except *dressing in a large bowl.*

If you like, season dressing with pepper. Drizzle dressing over salad, or serve it on the side!

> **HG FYI:** If you don't see any prepackaged no-salt-added turkey, check the deli counter. I'm a big fan of Boar's Head deli meats. You can also cook up your own skinless turkey breast with salt-free seasonings. (It'll take about 5 ounces raw turkey to yield 4 ounces cooked.) Or just get the turkey with the lowest sodium count you can find.

LUNCHES & DINNERS

The HG Chop Chop

326 calories, 7g fat, 432mg sodium, 35.5g carbs, 11g fiber, 19g sugars, 31.5g protein

4 cups chopped romaine or iceberg lettuce
4 ounces cooked and chopped skinless chicken breast or ready-to-eat shrimp
1 cup chopped cucumber
½ cup chopped red bell pepper
½ cup halved cherry tomatoes
½ cup peeled and chopped jicama
¼ cup chopped red onion
¼ cup canned sliced beets, drained and chopped
2 tablespoons vinegar (balsamic, red wine, white wine, rice, or cider)
1 teaspoon extra-virgin olive oil or grapeseed oil

In a large bowl, combine all ingredients except *vinegar and oil.*

Whisk vinegar with oil. Drizzle over salad, or serve it on the side!

> **HG Alternative:** Instead of vinegar, whisk oil with 1 serving (3 to 4 tablespoons) Sweet 'n Tangy Tomato Dressing, Creamy Cilantro Dressing, or Creamy Balsamic Dressing (page 196). So good! Sodium count will vary.

Leftover Beets Tip: For one of your snacks, make a salad of ⅓ cup sliced beets (drained), 1 cup chopped romaine or iceberg lettuce, and 1 cup high-volume veggies (page 111). Drizzle with 1½ teaspoons vinegar and 1 teaspoon extra-virgin olive oil or grapeseed oil.

LUNCHES & DINNERS

Big Burger with Side Salad

343 calories, 8.5g fat, 583mg sodium, 36.5g carbs, 9g fiber, 10.5g sugars, 33g protein

Burger

One 100-calorie flat sandwich bun

4 ounces raw extra-lean ground beef (4% fat or less)

1 tablespoon egg whites or fat-free liquid egg substitute

Dash each salt, black pepper, garlic powder, and onion powder

1 teaspoon ketchup

1 teaspoon mustard

1 lettuce leaf

1 large tomato slice

1 thin slice onion

Side Salad

1 cup lettuce

½ cup tomato, onion, or other high-fiber veggies (page 111)

½ cup cucumber, mushrooms, or other high-volume veggies (page 111)

2 ½ teaspoons vinegar (balsamic, red wine, white wine, rice, or cider)

½ teaspoon extra-virgin olive oil or grapeseed oil

Split bun into halves and, if you like, lightly toast.

In a medium bowl, thoroughly mix beef, egg whites, and seasonings. Evenly form into a 4-inch-wide patty.

LUNCHES & DINNERS

Big Burger with Side Salad (continued)

Bring a grill pan (or skillet) sprayed with nonstick spray to medium-high heat. Cook patty for 3 to 4 minutes per side, or until cooked to your preference.

Place patty on the bottom bun half. Top with remaining burger ingredients, followed by the top bun half.

Toss salad ingredients in a medium bowl, and serve alongside your burger!

The 411 on Turkey Swapping . . .

Lean ground turkey has more calories and fat than extra-lean ground beef, and *extra-lean* ground turkey can be a little dry and hard to find. You can make this meal with extra-lean ground turkey, if you'd like—just look for the kind with 150 calories or less and 5g fat or less per 4-ounce serving.

LUNCHES & DINNERS

Sloppy Jane Stir-Fry

339 calories, 6g fat, 700mg sodium, 31.5g carbs, 11g fiber, 16g sugars, 38.5g protein

3 cups bagged broccoli cole slaw
2/3 cup canned crushed tomatoes
1 tablespoon tomato paste
1 teaspoon brown sugar (not packed)
1 teaspoon Worcestershire sauce
1 teaspoon red wine vinegar
5 ounces raw extra-lean ground beef (4% fat or less)
Dash each salt, black pepper, chili powder, and paprika

Bring a large skillet sprayed with nonstick spray to medium-high heat. Add broccoli slaw and ½ cup water. Cover and cook until fully softened, 10 to 12 minutes. Uncover and, if needed, cook and stir until water has evaporated, 2 to 3 minutes.

Meanwhile, in a small bowl, mix all remaining ingredients except beef and seasonings.

Transfer slaw to a medium bowl, and blot away excess moisture. Remove skillet from heat, re-spray, and return to medium-high heat. Add beef and seasonings. Cook and crumble for 4 to 5 minutes, until fully cooked.

Add tomato mixture and slaw to the skillet and cook and stir until hot, about 2 minutes.

The Truth About Turkey . . .

Lean ground turkey has more calories and fat than extra-lean ground beef, and *extra-lean* ground turkey can be a little dry and hard to find. You can make this meal with extra-lean ground turkey, if you'd like—just look for the kind with 150 calories or less and 5g fat or less per 4-ounce serving.

LUNCHES & DINNERS

Chicken So Low Mein with Side Salad

303 calories, 7.5g fat, 775mg sodium, 33.5g carbs, 11g fiber, 15g sugars, 30.5g protein

Low Mein

1 bag House Foods Tofu Shirataki Spaghetti Shaped Noodle Substitute
1 tablespoon reduced-sodium/lite soy sauce
¾ teaspoon cornstarch
½ teaspoon granulated white sugar
1 cup frozen Asian-style stir-fry vegetables
1 cup bean sprouts
3 ounces cooked and chopped skinless chicken breast

Side Salad

1 cup lettuce
½ cup tomato, onion, or other high-fiber veggies (page 111)
½ cup cucumber, mushrooms, or other high-volume veggies (page 111)
2 teaspoons vinegar (balsamic, red wine, white wine, rice, or cider)
1 teaspoon extra-virgin olive oil or grapeseed oil

Use a strainer to rinse and drain noodles. Thoroughly pat dry. Roughly cut noodles.

To make the sauce, in a small bowl, combine soy sauce, cornstarch, and sugar. Add 2 tablespoons cold water, and stir until cornstarch dissolves.

Bring a wok (or skillet) sprayed with nonstick spray to medium-high heat. Add stir-fry veggies and bean sprouts. Cook and stir until hot, about 5 minutes.

Add noodles, chicken, and sauce. Cook and stir until hot and well mixed, about 4 minutes.

Toss salad ingredients in a medium bowl, and serve with low mein!

LUNCHES & DINNERS

Tuna Melt with Side Salad

343 calories, 11g fat, 594mg sodium, 33g carbs, 9g fiber, 8.5g sugars, 31.5g protein

Sandwich

One 100-calorie flat sandwich bun *or* 2 slices light bread

One 2.6-ounce pouch low-sodium tuna packed in water

1 tablespoon finely chopped red bell pepper

2 teaspoons light mayonnaise

1 teaspoon Hellmann's/Best Foods Dijonnaise (or creamy Dijon mustard)

1 large tomato slice

1 slice Sargento reduced-fat cheddar cheese

Side Salad

1 cup lettuce

½ cup tomato, onion, or other high-fiber veggies (page 111)

½ cup cucumber, mushrooms, or other high-volume veggies (page 111)

2 ½ teaspoons vinegar (balsamic, red wine, white wine, rice, or cider)

½ teaspoon extra-virgin olive oil or grapeseed oil

Toast bread slices or bun halves. Preheat oven or toaster oven to broil.

In a medium bowl, mix tuna, pepper, mayo, and Dijonnaise.

Evenly top one bun half/bread slice with tuna mixture, followed by tomato and cheese.

Broil until cheese has melted, 1 to 2 minutes. Top with the other bun half/bread slice.

LUNCHES & DINNERS

Tuna Melt with Side Salad (continued)

Toss salad ingredients in another medium bowl, and serve alongside your sandwich!

> **HG Alternative:** Don't have a toaster oven or just looking for a shortcut? Microwave the cheese-and-tuna-topped bun half/bread slice until cheese has melted, about 15 seconds.

> **HG FYI:** This recipe calls for Sargento cheese because of its impressively low sodium count. If you can't find Sargento, get the reduced-fat cheddar cheese with the lowest sodium count.

LUNCHES & DINNERS

Crunchy Beef Tacos with Side Salad

346 calories, 10.5g fat, 600mg sodium, 34.5g carbs, 5g fiber, 8g sugars, 29g protein

Tacos

4 ounces raw extra-lean ground beef (4% fat or less)

½ cup finely chopped brown mushrooms

2 tablespoons chopped onion

1 teaspoon taco seasoning mix

2 corn taco shells (flat bottomed, if available)

¼ cup shredded lettuce

2 tablespoons pico de gallo (or fresh salsa)

Salad

1 cup lettuce

1 cup cucumber, mushrooms, or other high-volume veggies (page 111)

2 tablespoons pico de gallo (or fresh salsa)

2 teaspoons vinegar (balsamic, red wine, white wine, rice, or cider)

Bring skillet sprayed with nonstick spray to medium-high heat. Add beef, mushrooms, and onion. Cook, stir, and crumble until beef is fully cooked and veggies have softened, about 5 minutes.

Sprinkle with taco seasoning, and continue to cook until any excess liquid has evaporated.

Evenly distribute mixture between taco shells, and top with lettuce and pico de gallo.

LUNCHES & DINNERS

Crunchy Beef Tacos with Side Salad (continued)

Toss salad ingredients in a medium bowl, and serve with tacos.

Let's Talk Turkey . . .

Lean ground turkey has more calories and fat than extra-lean ground beef, and *extra-lean* ground turkey can be a little dry and hard to find. You can make this meal with extra-lean ground turkey, if you'd like—just look for the kind with 150 calories or less and 5g fat or less per 4-ounce serving.

LUNCHES & DINNERS

Ginormous Tofu Stir-Fry

330 calories, 9g fat, 594mg sodium, 34.5g carbs, 9.5g fiber, 18.5g sugars, 29g protein

1 ½ teaspoons reduced-sodium/lite soy sauce

1 teaspoon oyster sauce

Dash ground ginger

Dash red pepper flakes

5 ounces block-style extra-firm tofu, cut into 1-inch cubes

Dash each garlic powder, onion powder, and black pepper

2 cups frozen Asian-style stir-fry vegetables

2 cups bean sprouts

1 ½ cups sliced mushrooms

¼ teaspoon chopped garlic

In a small bowl, combine soy sauce, oyster sauce, ginger, and red pepper flakes. Mix well.

Bring a large skillet sprayed with nonstick spray to high heat. Add tofu, and sprinkle with garlic powder, onion powder, and black pepper. Cook until golden brown, about 5 minutes, gently flipping to evenly brown.

Transfer tofu to a medium bowl, and cover to keep warm.

Reduce heat to medium high. Add stir-fry veggies, bean sprouts, mushrooms, and garlic to the skillet. Cover and cook until hot, about 5 minutes.

Give the sauce mixture a stir and add to the skillet, along with the tofu. Cook and stir until hot, about 1 minute.

LUNCHES & DINNERS

HG Tip! If you're vegetarian, look for vegetarian-friendly oyster sauce.

Leftover Tofu Tip: For one of your snacks, make a mini stir-fry . . .

Bring a skillet sprayed with nonstick spray to high heat. Add 2 ounces tofu, and sprinkle with seasonings. Cook until golden brown, about 5 minutes, gently flipping to evenly brown. Transfer to a medium bowl, and cover to keep warm.

Cook and stir 1 cup high-volume veggies (page 111) until softened. Add tofu and 1 tablespoon of sauce, dressing, or marinade with 25 calories or less. Mix well.

LUNCHES & DINNERS

Pizza-fied Chicken with Saucy Spaghetti Swap

356 calories, 5.5g fat, 762mg sodium, 34g carbs, 12g fiber, 14.5g sugars, 43g protein

⅔ cup canned crushed tomatoes

¾ teaspoon garlic powder

¾ teaspoon onion powder

¼ teaspoon black pepper, or more to taste

3 cups bagged broccoli cole slaw

One 4-ounce raw boneless skinless chicken breast cutlet, pounded to ½-inch thickness

¼ cup diced green bell pepper

¼ cup sliced mushrooms

2 tablespoons diced onion

2 tablespoons shredded part-skim mozzarella cheese

4 slices turkey pepperoni, chopped

1 teaspoon grated Parmesan cheese

Optional seasonings: red pepper flakes, oregano

Season tomatoes with ½ teaspoon garlic powder, ½ teaspoon onion powder, and ⅛ teaspoon black pepper.

Bring a large skillet sprayed with nonstick spray to medium-high heat. Add broccoli slaw and ½ cup water. Cover and cook until fully softened, 10 to 12 minutes. Uncover and, if needed, cook and stir until water has evaporated, 2 to 3 minutes. Transfer to a microwave-safe bowl, stir in ¾ths of the seasoned tomatoes, and cover to keep warm.

Remove skillet from heat, re-spray, and bring to medium heat. Season chicken with remaining ¼ teaspoon garlic powder, ¼ teaspoon onion powder, and ⅛ teaspoon black pepper. Cook for 5 minutes.

Flip chicken. Add bell pepper, mushrooms, and onion to the skillet. Stirring veggies occasionally, cook until veggies have slightly softened and chicken is cooked through, about 5 more minutes.

LUNCHES & DINNERS

Pizza-fied Chicken with Saucy Spaghetti Swap (continued)

Top chicken with remaining seasoned tomatoes, sprinkle with mozzarella cheese, and top with chopped pepperoni. Cover and cook for 1 minute, or until cheese has melted.

Plate your pizza-fied chicken, and top with cooked pepper, mushrooms, and onion. Sprinkle with Parmesan cheese.

If needed, reheat saucy slaw in the microwave.

> **HG Alternative:** Save time by steaming the slaw. Place it in a microwave-safe bowl with 2 tablespoons water. Cover and microwave for 3 minutes, or until soft. Drain excess liquid. Stir in the seasoned tomatoes, and microwave for 1 minute, or until hot. Cover to keep warm!

> **Leftover Pepperoni Tip:** As one of your snacks, pair 5 pieces of turkey pepperoni with 60 calories' worth of veggies!

> **Another Leftover Pepperoni Tip:** For one of your snacks, make a salad of 5 pieces chopped turkey pepperoni, 1 cup chopped romaine or iceberg lettuce, and 1 cup high-volume veggies (page 111). Drizzle with 1 ½ teaspoons vinegar and 1 teaspoon extra-virgin olive oil or grapeseed oil.

LUNCHES & DINNERS

Sesame-Ginger Salmon & Veggies

348 calories, 13g fat, 452mg sodium, 24.5g carbs, 6g fiber, 13.5g sugars, 27g protein

2 tablespoons low-fat sesame ginger dressing
⅛ teaspoon chopped garlic
Dash ground ginger
4 ounces raw skinless salmon
3 cups frozen Asian-style stir-fry vegetables

Preheat oven to 375 degrees. Lay a large piece of heavy-duty foil on a baking sheet and spray with nonstick spray.

In a wide bowl, mix dressing, garlic, and ginger. Add salmon and flip to coat. Cover and marinate in the fridge for 15 minutes.

Place stir-fry vegetables on the center of the foil and top with salmon. Drizzle with remaining marinade, and cover with another large piece of foil.

Fold together and seal all four edges of the foil pieces, forming a well-sealed packet. Bake for 30 minutes, or until salmon is cooked through and veggies are tender.

Cut packet to release steam before opening entirely.

> **Skillet Alternative:** Bring a large skillet sprayed with nonstick spray to medium heat. Add veggies to one half of the skillet and salmon to the other. Top veggies with garlic, and sprinkle salmon with ginger. Cook until veggies are hot and salmon is cooked through, about 8 minutes, stirring vegetables often and flipping salmon halfway through. Top with dressing.

LUNCHES & DINNERS

Grilled Cheese Platter

330 calories, 10.5g fat, 711mg sodium, 36g carbs, 11g fiber, 11g sugars, 25g protein

2 slices light bread
1 wedge The Laughing Cow Light Creamy Swiss cheese
1 slice Sargento reduced-fat cheddar cheese
2 teaspoons light whipped butter or light buttery spread
2 dashes garlic powder
2 cups raw or steamed sugar snap peas, red bell pepper, carrots, and/or other high-fiber veggies (page 111)
2 large hard-boiled egg whites

Lay bread slices flat, and spread both with cheese wedge. Top one slice with cheddar cheese and the other bread slice, cheesy side down. Spread the top of the sandwich with 1 teaspoon butter and sprinkle with a dash of garlic powder.

Bring a skillet sprayed with nonstick spray to medium heat. Place sandwich in the skillet, buttered side down. Spread the top with remaining 1 teaspoon butter, and sprinkle with remaining dash of garlic powder.

Cook until bread is lightly browned and cheese has melted, about 2 minutes per side. Serve with veggies and egg whites.

> **HG FYI:** This recipe calls for Sargento cheese because of its impressively low sodium count. If you can't find Sargento, get the reduced-fat cheddar cheese with the lowest sodium count.

Veggie-Steaming 411: Flip to page 110 for easy how-to advice!

LUNCHES & DINNERS

Chicken Fajita Tostadas

343 calories, 7.5g fat, 432mg sodium, 37.5g carbs, 7.5g fiber, 8.5g sugars, 33g protein

1 portabella mushroom cap, sliced
⅓ cup sliced bell pepper
⅓ cup sliced onion
4 ounces raw boneless skinless chicken breast, sliced
1 teaspoon fajita seasoning mix
Two 6-inch corn tortillas
¼ cup diced tomato
1 ounce (about 2 tablespoons) roughly mashed avocado
½ tablespoon chopped fresh cilantro
½ teaspoon lime juice
Dash salt

Optional seasoning: chili powder

Preheat oven to 375 degrees. Spray a baking sheet with nonstick spray.

Lay a square piece of heavy-duty foil on the baking sheet. Place sliced mushroom, pepper, and onion on the center of the foil. Season chicken with fajita seasoning, and place over the veggies.

Cover with another square piece of foil. Fold together and seal all four edges of the foil pieces, forming a well-sealed packet.

Lay tortillas on the sheet, next to the foil pack, and spray with nonstick spray. Bake for 5 minutes.

Flip tortillas. Bake until tortillas are crispy, about 5 more minutes.

LUNCHES & DINNERS

Chicken Fajita Tostadas (continued)

Transfer tortillas to a plate. Continue to bake the foil pack for 10 minutes, or until chicken is cooked through and veggies are tender.

Meanwhile, in a small bowl, combine tomato, avocado, cilantro, lime juice, salt and, if you like, chili powder. Mix well.

Cut packet to release steam before opening entirely.

Top tortillas with chicken-veggie mixture and tomato-avocado mixture. Yum!

Toaster Oven and Skillet Alternative! Toast tortillas in a toaster oven until lightly browned and crisp, about 5 minutes. Bring a large skillet sprayed with nonstick spray to medium heat. Add sliced mushroom, pepper, and onion. Cook and stir until slightly softened, about 4 minutes. Add chicken, seasoning mix, and 2 tablespoons water. Cook and stir until chicken is cooked through and veggies have softened, about 5 minutes.

Leftover Tortilla Tip: Make D.I.Y. Tortilla Chips (page 212)!

LUNCHES & DINNERS

Balsamic BBQ Chicken with Side Salad

337 calories, 7g fat, 467mg sodium, 37.5g carbs, 6g fiber, 20.5g sugars, 31g protein

Foil Pack

2 tablespoons BBQ sauce with about 45 calories per
    2-tablespoon serving
1 tablespoon balsamic vinegar
½ cup small broccoli florets
½ cup chopped onion
¼ cup frozen sweet corn kernels
One 4-ounce raw boneless skinless chicken breast cutlet,
    pounded to ½-inch thickness
½ teaspoon salt-free seasoning mix

Side Salad

1 cup lettuce
1 cup cucumber, mushrooms, or other high-volume
    veggies (page 111)
2 teaspoons vinegar (balsamic, red wine, white wine, rice,
    or cider)
1 teaspoon extra-virgin olive oil or grapeseed oil

Preheat oven to 375 degrees. Lay a large piece of heavy-duty foil on a baking sheet and spray with nonstick spray.

In a small bowl, mix BBQ sauce with balsamic vinegar.

Place broccoli, onion, and corn on the center of the foil. Season chicken with seasoning mix, and place over the veggies. Drizzle with BBQ-balsamic mixture. Cover with another large piece of foil.

LUNCHES & DINNERS

Balsamic BBQ Chicken with Side Salad (continued)

Fold together and seal all four edges of the foil pieces, forming a well-sealed packet. Bake for 25 minutes, or until chicken is cooked through and veggies are tender.

Cut packet to release steam before opening entirely.

Toss salad ingredients in a medium bowl, and serve with chicken and veggies.

> **Skillet Alternative!** In a small bowl, mix BBQ sauce with balsamic vinegar. Bring a large skillet sprayed with nonstick spray to medium heat. Add broccoli, onion, and corn to one half of the skillet, and add chicken to the other half. Cook until veggies have softened and chicken is cooked through, about 10 minutes, stirring veggies often and flipping chicken halfway through. Sprinkle chicken with salt-free seasoning, and drizzle with BBQ-balsamic mixture.

LUNCHES & DINNERS

Fruity Fish & Potato Foil Pack with Side Salad

329 calories, 7g fat, 334mg sodium, 35.5g carbs, 6g fiber, 12.5g sugars, 31g protein

Foil Pack

3 ounces baby red potatoes, cut into 1-inch pieces

5 ounces raw tilapia, cod, or sea bass

¼ teaspoon each garlic powder and chili powder

½ cup sliced red onion

¼ cup pineapple or mango salsa

Salad

1 cup lettuce

1 cup cucumber, mushrooms, or other high-volume
veggies (page 111)

2 teaspoons vinegar (balsamic, red wine, white wine, rice,
or cider)

1 teaspoon extra-virgin olive oil or grapeseed oil

Preheat oven to 375 degrees. Lay a large piece of heavy-duty foil on a baking sheet and spray with nonstick spray.

In a medium microwave-safe bowl, combine potatoes and 1 tablespoon water. Cover and microwave for 2 minutes, or until slightly softened. Drain excess water.

Place fish in the center of the foil, and surround with potatoes. Sprinkle with garlic powder and chili powder. Top fish with onion and salsa. Cover with another large piece of foil.

Fold together and seal all four edges of the foil pieces, forming a well-sealed packet. Bake for 15 minutes, or until fish and potatoes are cooked through.

LUNCHES & DINNERS

Fruity Fish & Potato Foil Pack with Side Salad (continued)

Cut packet to release steam before opening entirely.

Toss salad ingredients in a medium bowl, and serve with fish and potatoes.

> **HG Tip!** If your fish fillet is on the thin side, check it at 10 minutes.

For more tools for success—including an app that lets you create custom shopping lists and track your food—visit hungry-girl.com/diet!

LUNCHES & DINNERS

Faux-Fried Chicken Strips with Side Salad

347 calories, 8g fat, 472mg sodium, 34g carbs, 16.5g fiber, 4.5g sugars, 46.5g protein

Chicken Strips

½ cup Fiber One Original bran cereal

1 teaspoon salt-free seasoning mix

¼ cup egg whites or fat-free liquid egg substitute

6 ounces raw boneless skinless chicken breast, cut into 6 strips

1 tablespoon mustard

Side Salad

1 cup lettuce

1 cup cucumber, mushrooms, or other high-volume veggies (page 111)

2 teaspoons vinegar (balsamic, red wine, white wine, rice, or cider)

1 teaspoon extra-virgin olive oil or grapeseed oil

Preheat oven to 375 degrees. Spray a baking sheet with nonstick spray.

In a small blender or food processor, grind cereal into crumbs. (Or crush cereal with a meat mallet through a baggie.) Transfer to a wide bowl, and mix in seasoning mix.

Place egg whites or substitute in another wide bowl. One at a time, dunk chicken strips in egg, shake to remove excess, and coat with crumbs. Evenly lay on the baking sheet.

Bake for 8 minutes. Flip chicken. Bake until cooked through and crispy, about 6 minutes.

LUNCHES & DINNERS

Faux-Fried Chicken Strips with Side Salad (continued)

Toss salad ingredients in another medium bowl. Serve with chicken strips and mustard for dipping.

Fiber One 101 . . .

Fiber One is sweetened with aspartame. If you prefer a high-fiber cereal made without artificial sweeteners, use All-Bran Original.

If you have a small blender or food processor, use it. If not, crush your cereal in a sealable bag. Place it in the bag, squeeze out the air, and seal. Using the flat end of a meat mallet, pound the cereal through the bag on a flat surface. No mallet? A rolling pin or any heavy kitchen utensil with a flat surface will do.

LUNCHES & DINNERS

Chicken Parm with Saucy Pasta Swap

352 calories, 6g fat, 676mg sodium, 37g carbs, 16g fiber, 11g sugars, 43g protein

½ cup canned crushed tomatoes with basil

¼ teaspoon garlic powder

¼ teaspoon onion powder

3 cups bagged broccoli cole slaw

¼ cup Fiber One Original bran cereal, finely crushed

1 teaspoon Italian seasoning

2 tablespoons egg whites or fat-free liquid egg substitute

One 4-ounce raw boneless skinless chicken breast cutlet, pounded to ½-inch thickness

3 tablespoons shredded part-skim mozzarella cheese

Season tomatoes with ⅛ teaspoon garlic powder and ⅛ teaspoon onion powder (or more to taste).

Bring a large skillet sprayed with nonstick spray to medium-high heat. Add broccoli slaw and ½ cup water. Cover and cook until fully softened, 10 to 12 minutes. Uncover and, if needed, cook and stir until water has evaporated, 2 to 3 minutes. Transfer to a microwave-safe bowl, stir in ¾ths of the seasoned tomatoes, and cover to keep warm.

In a wide bowl, mix crushed cereal with Italian seasoning, remaining ⅛ teaspoon garlic powder, and remaining ⅛ teaspoon onion powder.

Place egg whites or substitute in another wide bowl. Coat chicken with egg, shake to remove excess, and coat with crumbs.

Re-spray skillet and return to medium heat. Cook chicken for 5 minutes per side, or until cooked through.

LUNCHES & DINNERS

Chicken Parm with Saucy Pasta Swap (continued)

Top chicken with remaining tomatoes, and sprinkle with cheese. Cover and cook for 2 minutes, or until cheese has melted.

If needed, reheat saucy slaw in the microwave.

HG Alternative: Save time by steaming the slaw. Place it in a microwave-safe bowl with 2 tablespoons water. Cover and microwave for 3 minutes, or until soft. Drain excess liquid. Stir in the seasoned tomatoes, and microwave for 1 minute, or until hot. Cover to keep warm!

HG Tip! If you can't find canned crushed tomatoes with basil, just use regular canned crushed tomatoes and add a little basil.

SNACKS

Savvy Snackin'!

There are so many snacks to choose from!
CRAVING-BUSTERS, PROTEIN POWERHOUSES,
DESSERT FIXES, HUGE PORTIONS . . . Experiment a little
to find the ones that are most satisfying for YOU.

Each of these snacks has 100 calories or less. And you get
THREE per day. Each snack also has less than 300mg sodium.
To keep your overall daily sodium intake in check, mix 'n
match sodium-free options like fruits and vegetables with
other snacks.

One of my favorite daily snack lineups? 2 ¼ cups chopped
watermelon + 100-calorie bag of 94% fat-free microwave
popcorn + 3 cups sugar snap peas. Yum! (But not all at
once!)

Check out the supplemental snacks on page 220 if you are
75 or more pounds overweight, have a vigorous exercise
routine, or find the approximate 1,300-calorie level too
aggressive for you.

And here's a great tip. ALWAYS keep a stash of smart
snacks at home, at work, and when you're on the go.
Flip to the Emergency Snack 101 section on page 56 for a
helpful guide.

Now turn the page . . . Happy snacking!

Snack Recipes

Supplemental Snacks

GRAB-N-GO SNACKS

* **100 calories' worth of fruit**
(see HG's Fruit Chart on page 192)

* **100 calories' worth of veggies**
(see HG's Veggie Chart on page 193)

* **60 calories' worth of veggies with 40 calories' worth of dip**
(see HG's Mix 'n Match Veggies & Dips on page 194)

* **½ ounce almonds or pistachios**
(about 12 almonds or 24 pistachios)

* **1 stick light string cheese with ¼ ounce almonds or pistachios**
(about 6 almonds or 12 pistachios)

* **1 stick light string cheese with *half* a 100-calorie serving of fruit**
(see HG's Fruit Chart on page 192)

  Try the string cheese at room temperature as opposed to straight out of the fridge . . . It's much better this way!

* **2 ounces (about 4 slices) no-salt-added turkey breast with 2 small cucumbers cut into spears**
PROTEIN POWERHOUSE!

* **100-calorie bag of 94% fat-free microwave popcorn**
HUGE PORTION!

  Jolly Time Healthy Pop, Orville Redenbacher's SmartPop!, Pop Secret 100 Calorie Pop

GRAB-N-GO SNACKS

* **Vitalicious VitaTop DESSERT FIX!**

VitaTops are all-natural, high-fiber, low-fat muffin tops with just 100 calories (or less) each. I love these! You can find the Deep Chocolate and a few other flavors at select markets (in the freezer aisle). You can also order online at Vitalicious.com.

* **Fiber One 90 Calorie Brownie or dessert bar CRAVING-BUSTER!**

* **6 ounces fat-free plain Greek yogurt PROTEIN POWERHOUSE!**

Fage Total 0%, Chobani 0%, Oikos 0%

*Add 1 no-calorie sweetener packet, if you like.

* **6 ounces fat-free flavored yogurt**

Yoplait Light (and Yoplait Greek 100)

Dannon Light & Fit (and Light & Fit Greek)

* **100-calorie bag (or 1 cup) freeze-dried fruit**

Funky Monkey, Just Tomatoes, Etc!

* **4 ounces fat-free flavored yogurt with ⅓ cup freeze-dried fruit**

GRAB-N-GO SNACKS

* **Low-fat frozen fudge pop or fruit bar with 100 calories or less DESSERT FIX!**

  Weight Watchers Giant, Skinny Cow, Healthy Choice Premium, Fudgsicles

  Blue Bunny FrozFruit, Fruitfull Juice Bars, Dreyer's/Edy's Fruit Bars

* **Enlightened The Good-For-You Ice Cream bar DESSERT FIX!**

* **100-calorie snack bar, cereal bar, or chewy granola bar**

  Quaker, Fiber One (especially Protein!), Special K

* **80 calories' worth of crackers (with fiber) with 1 tablespoon low-sugar preserves**

  Melba Toast, Melba Snacks, Ryvita, Wasa

  Smuckers Low Sugar

* **100-calorie bags (or pre-portioned) baked or popped chips CRAVING-BUSTER!**

  Popchips, Quaker Popped Chips, Kettle Brand Bakes

GRAB-N-GO SNACKS

* **10 mini rice cakes**
  (sweet and savory options, like caramel, apple cinnamon, cheddar, and BBQ)

* **5 mini rice cakes with *half* a 100-calorie serving of fruit**
  (see HG's Fruit Chart on page 192)

* **1 full-sized rice cake (50 calories or less) with *half* a 100-calorie serving of fruit**
  (see HG's Fruit Chart on page 192)

  Quaker rice cakes and mini rice cakes rock!

* **100-calories-or-less pouch of low-sodium tuna packed in water PROTEIN POWERHOUSE!**

  StarKist

* **SPECIAL SNACK: Quest Bars! PROTEIN POWERHOUSE!**
  I am OBSESSED with these! They taste incredible and are insanely filling, thanks to major amounts of protein and fiber. With around 200 calories per bar, have *half* of one as a snack, OR have a whole one in place of two snacks.

Download The Hungry Girl Diet App to create custom shopping lists and track your food! Visit hungry-girl.com/diet for details.

HG's Fruit Chart: 100-Calorie Portions!

Fruits with high fiber counts and large serving sizes tend to be the most filling. The stars represent HG favorites . . .

2 ¼ cups chopped watermelon (1.5g fiber)

2 cups halved strawberries; about 17 large strawberries (6g fiber)*

1 ¾ cups sliced apple; about 1 medium apple (4.5g fiber)*

1 ¾ cups chopped cantaloupe (2.5g fiber)

1 ⅔ cups blackberries (12.5g fiber)*

1 ⅔ cups sliced peaches; about 2 small peaches (4g fiber)

1 ⅔ cups chopped honeydew melon (2g fiber)

1 ½ cups raspberries (12g fiber)*

1 ½ cups sliced nectarines; about 1 ½ medium nectarines (3.5g fiber)

1 ¼ cups sliced pear; about 1 medium pear (5.5g fiber)

1 ¼ cups orange sections; 1 ½ medium oranges (5.5g fiber)*

1 ¼ cups blueberries (4.5g fiber)

1 ¼ cups chopped pineapple (3g fiber)

1 cup grapefruit sections; about 1 grapefruit (3.5g fiber)

1 cup cherries (3g fiber)

1 cup chopped mango; about ½ mango (2.5g fiber)

1 cup grapes; about 30 grapes (1.5g fiber)

¾ cup sliced banana; about 1 medium banana (3g fiber)

⅔ cup pomegranate arils; about ½ pomegranate (4.5g fiber)
   Look for 100-calorie containers of POM POMs, ready-to-eat arils!

3 clementines or other small mandarin oranges (3.5g fiber)

2 tangerines or other medium mandarin oranges (3.5g fiber)

HG's Veggie Chart: 100-Calorie Portions!

High fiber counts and large serving sizes . . . YAY!

1 extra-large artichoke (11g fiber)

4 ½ cups chopped cabbage (10g fiber)

4 cups (one 12-oz. bag) broccoli cole slaw (12g fiber)

4 cups sliced bell peppers (7g fiber)

3 ½ cups asparagus pieces (10g fiber)

3 ½ cups cauliflower florets (7.5g fiber)

3 ½ cups cherry or grape tomatoes (6g fiber)

3 ⅓ cups sugar snap peas (5.5g fiber)

3 cups broccoli florets (7g fiber)

3 cups chopped kale (7g fiber)

2 ½ cups Brussels sprouts (8.5g fiber)

2 ¼ cups jicama sticks (13g fiber)

2 ¼ cups cooked spaghetti squash (5g fiber)

1 ½ cups cubed butternut squash (4g fiber)

28 baby carrots (8g fiber)

*Measurements are for raw vegetables
(unless otherwise indicated).*

HG FYI: Flip to page 198 to learn how to bake or steam spaghetti squash!

HG's Mix 'n Match Veggies & Dips

60-Calorie Veggie Portions

1 medium artichoke (7g fiber)

2 ¾ cups chopped cabbage (6g fiber)

2 ½ cups bagged broccoli cole slaw (7.5g fiber)

2 ½ cups sliced bell peppers (4.5g fiber)

2 ¼ cups asparagus pieces (6g fiber)

2 ¼ cups cherry or grape tomatoes (4g fiber)

2 cups broccoli florets (4.5g fiber)

2 cups cauliflower florets (4g fiber)

2 cups sugar snap peas (3.5g fiber)

1 ¾ cups chopped kale (4g fiber)

1 ½ cups Brussels sprouts (5g fiber)

1 ½ cups cooked spaghetti squash (3g fiber)

1 ¼ cups jicama sticks (7.5g fiber)

1 cup cubed butternut squash (2.5g fiber)

17 baby carrots (5g fiber)

*Measurements are for raw vegetables
(unless otherwise indicated).*

HG's Mix 'n Match Veggies & Dips

Dips (and More) with 40 Calories or Less

* 1 serving (3 to 4 tablespoons) Sweet 'n Tangy Tomato Dressing, Creamy Cilantro Dressing, or Creamy Balsamic Dressing (page 196)

* ¼ cup fresh salsa or pico de gallo

* 1 ½ tablespoons hummus

Toss cooked veggies with . . .

* ½ cup canned crushed tomatoes, seasoned with garlic powder, onion powder, etc.

* ¼ cup low-fat marinara sauce

* 1 tablespoon of any sauce, dressing, or marinade with 25 calories or less per 1-tablespoon serving

* 2 teaspoons light whipped butter or light buttery spread

Look for options with 250mg sodium or less.

HG Dips and Dressings

Pair with a 60-Calorie Veggie Portion as a snack, or use in salad and sandwich platter recipes as directed . . .

Sweet 'n Tangy Tomato Dip/Dressing

24 calories, 0g fat, 220mg sodium, 5g carbs, 1g fiber, 3g sugars, 0.5g protein

3 tablespoons canned crushed tomatoes
1 teaspoon seasoned rice vinegar
1 teaspoon finely chopped basil
⅛ teaspoon garlic powder

Combine and mix well.

Creamy Cilantro Dip/Dressing

30 calories, 0g fat, 168mg sodium, 2.5g carbs, 0g fiber, 2g sugars, 4.5g protein

3 tablespoons fat-free plain Greek yogurt
1 tablespoon water
1 teaspoon finely chopped cilantro
½ teaspoon lime juice
⅛ teaspoon each cumin, garlic powder, onion powder
Dash each salt and black pepper

Combine and mix well.

Creamy Balsamic Dip/Dressing

31 calories, 0g fat, 13mg sodium, 4g carbs, 0g fiber, 3g sugars, 3g protein

2 tablespoons fat-free plain Greek yogurt
1 tablespoon balsamic vinegar
Half a no-calorie sweetener packet

Combine and mix well.

Big Batch of Sweet 'n Tangy Tomato Dip/Dressing

⅛th of recipe (about 3 tablespoons): 24 calories, 0g fat, 220mg sodium, 5g carbs, 1g fiber, 3g sugars, 0.5g protein

1 ½ cups canned crushed tomatoes
2 tablespoons plus 2 teaspoons seasoned rice vinegar
2 tablespoons plus 2 teaspoons finely chopped basil
1 teaspoon garlic powder

Combine ingredients in a sealable container. Mix well.

Big Batch of Creamy Cilantro Dip/Dressing

⅛th of recipe (about ¼ cup): 30 calories, 0g fat, 168mg sodium, 2.5g carbs, 0g fiber, 2g sugars, 4.5g protein

1 ½ cups fat-free plain Greek yogurt
½ cup water
2 tablespoons plus 2 teaspoons finely chopped cilantro
1 tablespoon plus 1 teaspoon lime juice
1 teaspoon each cumin, garlic powder, onion powder
½ teaspoon salt and black pepper

Combine ingredients in a sealable container. Mix well.

Big Batch of Creamy Balsamic Dip/Dressing

⅛th of recipe (about 3 tablespoons): 31 calories, 0g fat, 13mg sodium, 4g carbs, 0g fiber, 3g sugars, 3g protein

1 cup fat-free plain Greek yogurt
½ cup balsamic vinegar
4 no-calorie sweetener packets

Combine ingredients in a sealable container. Mix well.

Veggie 411!

Prefer your veggies cooked? Keep reading . . .

How to Steam Veggies in the Microwave . . .

For 1 to 3 cups of most veggies . . .

Place veggies in a microwave-safe bowl with 2 tablespoons water. Cover and microwave for about 3 minutes, until softened. Repeat as needed. Drain or blot dry.

How to Bake Spaghetti Squash . . .

Preheat oven to 400 degrees.

Microwave squash for 3 to 4 minutes, until soft enough to cut. Halve lengthwise; scoop out and discard seeds. Fill a large baking pan with ½ inch water and place squash halves in the pan, cut sides down.

Bake until tender, about 40 minutes. (Check it at 30 minutes, if you like it on the firm side.)

Use a fork to scrape out squash strands. Place in a strainer to drain excess moisture. Blot dry, if needed!

How to Microwave Spaghetti Squash . . .

Microwave squash for 3 to 4 minutes, until soft enough to cut. Slice into quarters. Scoop out and discard seeds.

Place one piece of squash in a wide microwave-safe bowl, cut side down. Add 2 tablespoons water, cover, and cook for 8 minutes, or until soft. Repeat with remaining squash.

Use a fork to scrape out squash strands. Place in a strainer to drain excess moisture. Blot dry, if needed!

How to Cook Broccoli Cole Slaw or Chopped Cabbage in a Skillet . . .

Bring a large skillet sprayed with nonstick spray to medium-high heat. Add slaw or cabbage and ½ cup water.

Cover and cook until fully softened, 10 to 12 minutes. Uncover and, if needed, cook and stir until water has evaporated, 2 to 3 minutes.

SPEEDY SNACKS!

Baked Kale Chips CRAVING-BUSTER!

98 calories, 2g fat, 231mg sodium, 17.5g carbs, 7g fiber,
4.5g sugars, 8.5g protein

*Preheat oven to 425 degrees. Place 3 cups kale leaves on a
baking sheet sprayed with nonstick spray. Spritz with nonstick
spray, and sprinkle with a dash of salt. Bake until crispy,
5 to 7 minutes. Yum!*

Easy Cheesy Noodles CRAVING-BUSTER!

55 calories, 2.5g fat, 210mg sodium, 7g carbs, 4g fiber,
1g sugars, 2.5g protein

*Use a strainer to rinse, drain, and pat dry 1 bag House Foods
Tofu Shirataki Fettuccine Shaped Noodle Substitute. Roughly
cut, and microwave for 1 minute. Thoroughly pat dry. Add
1 wedge The Laughing Cow Light Creamy Swiss cheese,
breaking it into pieces. Microwave for 1 minute. Stir and
season to taste.*

Veggie Egg Mug PROTEIN POWERHOUSE!

83 calories, 0g fat, 252mg sodium, 6g carbs, 1g fiber,
3g sugars, 14.5g protein

*In a large microwave-safe mug sprayed with nonstick spray,
combine ½ cup chopped spinach with 2 tablespoons each
chopped onion and bell pepper. Microwave for 1 ½ minutes,
or until softened. Blot away moisture, add ½ cup egg whites
or fat-free liquid egg substitute, and stir. Microwave for 1
minute. Stir in 2 tablespoons chopped tomato, and microwave
for 1 minute, or until set.*

SPEEDY SNACKS!

Deli Rolls PROTEIN POWERHOUSE!

64 calories, 0.5g fat, 138mg sodium, 6g carbs, 2g fiber,
3.5g sugars, 9g protein

*Place 2 large lettuce leaves on a plate. Top each with ½ ounce
(about 1 slice) no-salt-added turkey breast, 2 medium tomato
slices, and ½ teaspoon mustard (yellow, Dijon, or honey).*

Feta-Stuffed Strawberries HUGE PORTION!

100 calories, 4.5g fat, 260mg sodium, 11.5g carbs, 3g fiber,
7g sugars, 5.5g protein

*Slice stem ends off 8 large strawberries, about ½ inch,
revealing an opening in each berry. Use a narrow spoon to
remove about half of the flesh inside each berry, allowing
room for filling. Evenly fill with 3 tablespoons crumbled
reduced-fat feta cheese, breaking crumbles into smaller
pieces if needed. Eat!*

Upside-Down Cream Pie DESSERT FIX!

88 calories, <0.5g fat, 92mg sodium, 16.5g carbs, 0.5g fiber,
12.5g sugars, 4.5g protein

*Crush 1 low-fat honey graham cracker (¼ sheet). Sprinkle it
over 4 ounces (about ½ cup) fat-free flavored yogurt.*

SPEEDY SNACKS!

Berry-Citrus Slush DESSERT FIX!

94 calories, 0.5g fat, 6mg sodium, 23g carbs, 5g fiber, 14.5g sugars, 1g protein

In a blender, combine 1 cup unsweetened frozen mixed berries (partially thawed), ½ cup Trop50 No Pulp, and 1 no-calorie sweetener packet. Add ¾ cup crushed ice, and pulse until smooth (stopping and stirring, if needed).

EZ Caprese-Style Salad HUGE PORTION!

95 calories, 3g fat, 200mg sodium, 8.5g carbs, 2.5g fiber, 4.5g sugars, 8.5g protein

Slice a stick of light string cheese into ¼-inch coins. Toss with 2 cups chopped romaine or iceberg lettuce, ¼ cup chopped tomato, 2 tablespoons chopped fresh basil, and 1 tablespoon balsamic vinegar.

Parmed-Up Broccoli HUGE PORTION!

100 calories, 3g fat, 207mg sodium, 12g carbs, 4.5g fiber, 3g sugars, 9g protein

Place 2 cups broccoli florets in a microwave-safe bowl with 2 tablespoons water. Cover and microwave for 3 minutes, or until soft. Drain excess liquid, and sprinkle with 1 tablespoon grated Parmesan cheese.

SPEEDY SNACKS!

Apple Pie in a Mug DESSERT FIX!

72 calories, <0.5g fat, 1mg sodium, 19g carbs, 3.5g fiber, 13g sugars, <0.5g protein

Place 1 cup chopped apple, ½ teaspoon cinnamon, ⅛ teaspoon lemon juice, and 1 no-calorie sweetener packet in a microwave-safe mug sprayed with nonstick spray. Mix well. Cover and microwave for 2 minutes, or until softened.

Tuna Lettuce Wraps PROTEIN POWERHOUSE!

99 calories, 1.5g fat, 232mg sodium, 2.7g carbs, 1g fiber, 0.5g sugars, 17g protein

Mix one 2.6-ounce pouch low-sodium tuna packed in water with 2 teaspoons Dijonnaise. Divide between 2 large lettuce leaves.

Tuna-Stuffed Egg Whites PROTEIN POWERHOUSE!

82 calories, 1.5g fat, 175mg sodium, 1g carbs, <0.5g fiber, 0.5g sugars, 14.5g protein

Mix 1 ounce low-sodium tuna packed in water (drained), 1 teaspoon light mayo, and a dash each garlic powder, onion powder, and black pepper. Slice 2 large hard-boiled eggs in half, and discard yolks. Distribute tuna among egg-white halves, and then eat.

SNACK RECIPES

Souper-Sized Soup HUGE PORTION!

¼th of recipe (about 2 cups): 93 calories, 0.5g fat,
205mg sodium, 18g carbs, 4.5g fiber, 8g sugars, 5g protein

1 cup chopped carrots

1 cup chopped onion

1 tablespoon chopped garlic

6 cups low-sodium chicken, vegetable, or beef broth

3 cups chopped green cabbage

1 cup chopped green beans

1 cup chopped zucchini

2 tablespoons tomato paste

1 teaspoon dried basil

½ teaspoon dried oregano

½ teaspoon black pepper, or more to taste

Bring a large nonstick pot to medium heat. Add carrots, onion, and garlic, and cook and stir until onion has softened, about 5 minutes.

Carefully add all remaining ingredients. Bring to a boil, and then reduce to a simmer.

Cover and cook for 15 minutes, or until green beans are tender.

MAKES 4 SERVINGS

SNACK RECIPES

Double-Strawberry Smoothie DESSERT FIX!

97 calories, 0g fat, 55mg sodium, 21.5g carbs, 2.5g fiber, 14g sugars, 4g protein

3 ounces (about ⅓ cup) fat-free strawberry yogurt
¾ cup frozen unsweetened strawberries, partly thawed
1 no-calorie sweetener packet
1 cup crushed ice *or* 5 to 8 ice cubes

Place all ingredients in a blender. Add 2 tablespoons cold water, and blend at high speed until smooth. (If needed, turn off the blender, stir, and blend again.)

SNACK RECIPES

Lean 'n Green Sipper HUGE PORTION!

100 calories, 0.5g fat, 25mg sodium, 24.5g carbs, 3.5g fiber, 14g sugars, 3g protein

¾ cup chopped seedless cucumber

¾ cup chopped kale

½ cup chopped Granny Smith apple

¼ cup frozen green seedless grapes

1 no-calorie sweetener packet

½ teaspoon lemon juice

1 cup crushed ice *or* 5 to 8 ice cubes

Blend all ingredients with ⅓ cup cold water, stopping and stirring if needed.

SNACK RECIPES

Lord of the Onion Strings CRAVING-BUSTER!

100 calories, 0.5g fat, 278mg sodium, 27g carbs, 9g fiber, 8g sugars, 5g protein

¼ cup Fiber One Original bran cereal, finely crushed
¼ teaspoon garlic powder
⅛ teaspoon onion powder
Dash black pepper
¾ cup thinly sliced onion (a.k.a. onion strings)
2 tablespoons fat-free liquid egg substitute
1 tablespoon ketchup

Preheat oven to 375 degrees. Spray a baking sheet with nonstick spray.

In a large bowl, mix crushed cereal with seasonings.

Place onion strings in a bowl, top with egg substitute, and toss to coat.

Shaking off any excess egg substitute, transfer half of the onion strings to the cereal crumbs. Gently toss to coat. Transfer to the baking sheet, and spread them out a bit. Repeat with remaining onion strings.

Bake until outsides are crispy and insides are soft, 10 to 15 minutes.

Serve with ketchup for dipping.

Fiber One 101 . . .

Fiber One is sweetened with aspartame. If you prefer a high-fiber cereal made without artificial sweeteners, use All-Bran Original.

Crush your cereal in a sealable bag. Place it in the bag, squeeze out the air, and seal. Using the flat end of a meat mallet, pound the cereal through the bag on a flat surface. No mallet? A rolling pin or any heavy kitchen utensil with a flat surface will do.

SNACK RECIPES

Cheesy Faux-tato Skins CRAVING-BUSTER!

96 calories, 5g fat, 184mg sodium, 8g carbs, 2g fiber, 5g sugars, 8g protein

1 medium zucchini, stem ends removed
3 tablespoons shredded reduced-fat Mexican-blend or cheddar cheese
1 tablespoon diced tomato
1 teaspoon chopped scallions

Pierce zucchini several times with a fork. Place on a microwave-safe plate, and microwave for 2 minutes.

Flip zucchini and microwave for 2 more minutes, or until softened.

Let cool, about 5 minutes. Cut zucchini in half lengthwise. Gently scoop out and discard the inside flesh, leaving about ¼ inch inside the skin. Thoroughly pat dry.

Sprinkle cheese in the hollowed-out zucchini halves.

Microwave for 30 seconds, or until cheese has melted.

Cut each piece in half widthwise, and sprinkle with tomato and scallions.

SNACK RECIPES

Snack-tastic Butternut Fries CRAVING-BUSTER!

96 calories, <0.5g fat, 294mg sodium, 24.5g carbs, 3.5g fiber, 7.5g sugars, 1.5g protein

6 ounces peeled butternut squash, cut into
   French-fry-shaped spears
Dash coarse salt
1 tablespoon ketchup

Preheat oven to 425 degrees. Spray a baking sheet with nonstick spray.

Thoroughly pat dry the squash spears. Lay them on the sheet, and sprinkle with salt. Bake for 10 minutes.

Flip spears and bake until mostly tender on the inside and crispy on the outside, about 6 minutes.

Serve with ketchup for dipping!

HG Squash Tips!

* Choose a squash that's mostly long and narrow with a short round section. The round part is hollow and full of seeds; the long section is solid squash, perfect for cutting into spears.

* If the squash is too firm to cut, pop it in the microwave for a minute to soften it.

* Consider cutting up the entire squash at once. Then store the remaining spears in a covered container in the fridge.

SNACK RECIPES

Easy Baked Carrot Fries CRAVING-BUSTER!

100 calories, 0.5g fat, 298mg sodium, 23.5g carbs, 5.5g fiber, 13g sugars, 1.5g protein

7 ounces peeled carrots (about 1 ½ large carrots), cut into French-fry-shaped spears
1 tablespoon ketchup

Preheat oven to 400 degrees. Spray a baking sheet with nonstick spray.

Lay spears on the sheet. Bake for 15 minutes.

Flip spears. Bake until tender on the inside and slightly crispy on the outside, about 10 more minutes.

Serve with ketchup for dipping!

SNACK RECIPES

Perfect Pizza-bella CRAVING-BUSTER!

100 calories, 3g fat, 263mg sodium, 8.5g carbs, 2.5g fiber, 4.5g sugars, 10.5g protein

1 stick light string cheese
1 portabella mushroom, stem removed and reserved
2 tablespoons canned crushed tomatoes

Seasonings: garlic powder, onion powder, Italian seasoning, red pepper flakes

Preheat oven to 400 degrees. Spray a baking sheet with nonstick spray.

Break string cheese stick into thirds and place in a blender or food processor; blend at high speed until shredded. (Or pull into shreds and roughly chop.)

Place mushroom cap on the sheet, rounded side down. Bake until slightly tender, about 8 minutes.

Meanwhile, finely chop mushroom stem. In a small bowl, stir into crushed tomatoes.

Remove sheet, but leave oven on. Blot away excess moisture from mushroom cap.

Evenly top mushroom cap with crushed tomato mixture, and season with spices. Sprinkle with cheese and, if you like, additional spices.

Bake until mushroom is tender, tomatoes are hot, and cheese has melted, 8 to 10 minutes.

SNACK RECIPES

D.I.Y. Tortilla Chips CRAVING-BUSTER!

100 calories, 1.5g fat, 168mg sodium, 20.5g carbs, 2g fiber, 1g sugars, 2g protein

Two 6-inch corn tortillas
Dash salt

Preheat oven to 400 degrees. Spray a baking sheet lightly with nonstick spray.

Cut tortillas in half. Cut each half into 3 triangles, for a total of 12 triangles.

Place tortilla triangles close together on the sheet. Spray with nonstick spray, and sprinkle with salt.

Bake for 5 minutes. Carefully flip triangles and bake until crispy, 3 to 5 minutes.

SNACK RECIPES

Upside-Down Strawberry Pie DESSERT FIX!

100 calories, 1g fat, 41mg sodium, 28.5g carbs, 8.5g fiber, 12.5g sugars, 2g protein

1 cup chopped strawberries
1 tablespoon low-sugar strawberry preserves
3 tablespoons Fiber One Original bran cereal, lightly crushed
2 dashes cinnamon

In a medium bowl, mix strawberries with preserves.

In a small bowl, mix crushed cereal with cinnamon. Sprinkle mixture over strawberries.

Fiber One is sweetened with aspartame. If you prefer a high-fiber cereal made without artificial sweeteners, use All-Bran Original.

SNACK RECIPES

Cheesy Turkey Rollups PROTEIN POWERHOUSE!

94 calories, 2g fat, 219mg sodium, 3.5g carbs, 0.5g fiber, 2.5g sugars, 13.5g protein

1 ½ ounces (about 3 slices) no-salt-added turkey breast
1 wedge The Laughing Cow Light Creamy Swiss cheese
6 strips red bell pepper

Spread turkey slices with cheese, and top each with pepper strips. Roll up.

HG FYI: *If you don't see any prepackaged no-salt-added turkey, check the deli counter. I love the kind by Boar's Head. Or just get the turkey with the lowest sodium count you can find.*

SNACK RECIPES

Sweet 'n Crunchy Chinese Slaw SWEET & SAVORY!

¼th of recipe (1 heaping cup): 75 calories, 1g fat,
252mg sodium, 14.5g carbs, 3.5g fiber, 9g sugars, 2.5g protein

One 12-ounce bag (about 4 cups) broccoli cole slaw
⅓ cup low-fat sesame ginger dressing
⅔ cup mandarin orange segments packed in juice, drained
   and chopped
½ cup canned sliced water chestnuts, drained and chopped
¼ cup chopped scallions

Toss slaw with dressing, and stir in remaining ingredients.
Refrigerate for at least 1 hour.

MAKES 4 SERVINGS

SNACK RECIPES

Magical Margarita Light CRAVING-BUSTER!

99 calories, 0g fat, 89mg sodium, 2.5g carbs, 0g fiber, 0.5g sugars, 0.5g protein

This one is more of a special-occasion, adults-only treat than a snack . . .

6 ounces (¾ cup) diet lemon-lime soda
1 ¼ ounces (2 ½ tablespoons) tequila
1 ounce (2 tablespoons) lime juice
One single-serving or two-serving packet (makes 16 ounces lemonade) sugar-free lemonade powdered drink mix
1 cup crushed ice *or* 5 to 8 ice cubes

Optional garnish: lime slice

In a glass or shaker, combine all ingredients except *ice. Stir until drink mix has dissolved.*

Fill a margarita glass with ice, pour, and enjoy! (Or blend it all in a blender.)

This cocktail can be made with natural ingredients! Look for stevia-sweetened soda and drink mix, like Blue Sky Zero Soda and True Lemonade.

Don't miss the Happy Hour section on page 78, for more plan-friendly cocktails!

SNACK RECIPES

Chocolate-Chip-Stuffed Strawberries DESSERT FIX!

96 calories, 3.5g fat, 42mg sodium, 14g carbs, 2g fiber,
9.5g sugars, 3.5g protein

5 large strawberries
2 tablespoons light/low-fat ricotta cheese
1 no-calorie sweetener packet
1 drop vanilla extract
1 ½ teaspoons mini semi-sweet chocolate chips

Slice the stem ends off the strawberries, about ½ inch, revealing an opening in each berry. Use a narrow spoon to remove about half of the flesh inside each berry, allowing room for filling.

In a small bowl, mix ricotta, sweetener, and vanilla extract until uniform.

Spoon ricotta mixture into a bottom corner of a plastic bag; snip off the tip of that corner to create a small hole, and pipe the mixture through the hole into the strawberries. Top with chocolate chips.

SNACK RECIPES

Caramel Apple Crunchcake DESSERT FIX!

97 calories, 1.5g fat, 75mg sodium, 17.5g carbs, 1g fiber,
7.5g sugars, 3.5g protein

2 tablespoons light/low-fat ricotta cheese
1 no-calorie sweetener packet
1 drop vanilla extract
1 full-sized caramel-flavored rice cake
¼ cup thinly sliced apple
Dash cinnamon

*In a small bowl, mix ricotta, sweetener, and vanilla extract
until uniform.*

*Spread ricotta mixture onto the rice cake. Top with apple and
cinnamon. Yum!*

SNACK RECIPES

Cannoli Bites DESSERT FIX!

97 calories, 3g fat, 147mg sodium, 14g carbs, 0.5g fiber, 7g sugars, 4.5g protein

2 ½ tablespoons light/low-fat ricotta cheese
1 no-calorie sweetener packet
1 drop vanilla extract
1 teaspoon mini semi-sweet chocolate chips
4 caramel-flavored mini rice cakes

In a medium bowl, mix ricotta, sweetener, and vanilla extract until uniform. Stir in chocolate chips.

Spread ricotta mixture onto the rice cakes. Eat!

Supplemental Snacks

If you are 75 or more pounds overweight, have a vigorous exercise routine, or feel the approximate 1,300-calorie level is too aggressive for you, consider adding one of the following supplemental snacks to your day (in addition to your three daily snacks) . . .

* 100 calories' worth of fruit (see HG's Fruit Chart on page 192) with 6 ounces fat-free plain Greek yogurt

* 100 calories' worth of fruit (see HG's Fruit Chart on page 192) with ½ ounce almonds or pistachios (about 12 almonds or 24 pistachios)

* 3 ounces (about 6 slices) no-salt-added turkey breast with 100 calories' worth of veggies (see HG's Veggie Chart on page 193)

LIFE AFTER THE FOUR-WEEK PLAN!
(CONTINUED WEIGHT LOSS, MAINTENANCE, AND SURVIVAL STRATEGIES)

CONGRATULATIONS!

You've completed the four-week plan.
Wondering what to do now? Keep reading . . .

More weight to lose?

You can continue following the plan for as long as you'd like until reaching your goal weight. You can start back at Week 1 (to reinvigorate your weight-loss journey), continuously repeat Week 4 (the most flexible), or pick it up anywhere in between.

Another option is to follow a modified version of the plan, using new skills you've sharpened, meal ideas you've come to love, and more. Simply count calories, aiming for the same 1,300-calories-per-day as the plan. (Or 1,500 calories, if you've been having the supplemental snacks.) You can also use HG recipes and snack suggestions to make those 1,300 calories satisfying and delicious!

A third option is to use HG recipes, snack ideas, meal techniques, etc., in conjunction with any diet that allows you to be flexible with your food choices. The Hungry Girl universe is filled with options, so you can choose foods that help you stay at or below a specified daily target.

If you're not already a subscriber, sign up for free daily emails at hungry-girl.com! The newsletters are packed with food finds, new recipes, and so much more . . . All excellent tools for modified versions of the plan.

To maintain your weight loss . . .

For maintenance, we suggest you continue to count calories. Use Hungry Girl recipes, food finds, and survival strategies to make maintaining easy and fun! In fact, the entire next section of the book is filled with tips, tricks, and strategies to help you maintain a healthy weight in a realistic and enjoyable way.

One way to find a ballpark estimate of the calories you need to maintain your weight is to multiply it by 10. So, for example, if you weigh 150 pounds, 1,500 calories per day is your estimate. However, it's not a good idea to dip below 1,200 calories per day. And keep in mind that personal metabolism and activity level can affect how many calories you need to maintain your new weight.

To find your individual calorie needs for maintenance, try one week at the calorie level determined by the above method. (If this level is lower than what you consumed on the plan— 1,300 to 1,500 calories—stay at the number of calories you consumed on the plan.) If you continue to lose weight, increase by 100 calories and stay at that level for a week. If you gain weight, decrease by 100 calories and stay at that level for a week. Continue increasing or decreasing, as needed, until you find your ideal intake for maintenance.

Don't want to diligently count calories forever? Use the 80/20 rule, making smart choices the majority of the time and loosening up the reins the other 20 percent. This way, you'll always have some wiggle room and flexibility without throwing off your weight-management goals. If you notice your clothes fitting tighter or the number on the scale going up, start paying closer attention to the exact number of calories you're consuming.

CALORIE COUNTING 101

If you've decided to count calories, you may be wondering how exactly to go about it. Good news! There are so many great resources out there ready to give you the info you need. Here's a crash course to get you started . . .

Online Nutritional Databases
Calorie Count and CalorieKing are just a couple of the easy-to-use resources out there. They're crammed with nutritional information on hundreds of thousands of foods, from fruits and vegetables to the brand-name products on supermarket shelves. Both also offer mobile apps, so you can count calories (and fat, carbs, sodium, etc.) on the go.

Restaurant Nutritional Info
Many restaurants provide nutrition stats for menu items, either on location or on their website. And many chains are actually required to disclose this information, which is great news for consumers. Some even have calorie counts listed right on the menus. If you're heading out to dinner, start by checking out a restaurant's website for this information. If you're not able to check in advance and don't see calorie counts on the menu, ask if they have a nutritional pamphlet available for you to see. For specific restaurant survival strategies, flip to the Dining Out Survival Guides, starting on page 244!

Nutritional Panels (and Need-to-Know Label Info!)
It seems like a no-brainer, but it's actually frighteningly easy to misread product labels. First of all, don't be swayed by some of the more misleading front-of-the-package claims. Just because something is "organic," "made with whole grains," or "reduced fat," doesn't mean it is low in calories or diet friendly in any way. Flip over the package for the hard facts. The single biggest mistake people make when reading labels is assuming that the "per serving" stats listed are for the entire package. You might be holding a product that *looks* like a single serving, only to find out it contains 2.5 servings . . . which means all those numbers have to be multiplied accordingly, or you need to measure out a single portion and stick to it.

ADJUSTING TO WEIGHT MAINTENANCE

Loosen the reins a little, but keep things familiar.
A lot of people rely on careful calorie counting while losing weight to keep the number on the scale moving down. But since maintaining weight is a lifelong goal, it's important to find an approach that you can really, well, *maintain*! When you're finished with the plan, it helps to have a slew of go-to guilt-free dishes with similar stats, both at home and at restaurants. This way, you won't have to overthink things or calculate calorie counts on a regular basis. The meals in this plan (including those in the Dining Out on the Plan section on page 98) can be incorporated seamlessly into a maintenance routine.

Check in . . . with yourself. Be accountable and honest with yourself. Maybe you don't have to weigh in each week, but if you notice your jeans are starting to get a bit tight, it's probably time to step on a scale and step up your maintenance efforts. You might even want to give yourself a monthly weigh-in date, like the first of the month, so you're less likely to let things go without realizing it.

Keep health a priority. Maintaining your goal weight can be harder than losing the weight because you don't have the motivation of seeing a lower number on the scale to keep you going. But the ultimate goal is to get healthy and stay healthy. Even if you aren't cutting calories and doing calorie-burning cardio sessions, you can still make nutritious choices and try to get in some physical activity every day.

THE 80/20 RULE

It's all about a realistic approach to eating smart. If you make good choices most of the time, you can be a little more flexible other times. This way, you won't feel restricted but you won't go overboard either. Making perfect food choices 100 percent of the time (forever!) isn't a realistic goal for most people, and if you tell yourself that you have to do it, you'll be more likely to get discouraged and give up after a "bad" meal or day.

Actually, 80/20 is more of a concept than a hard-and-fast rule. If you adopt the idea, it sort of works itself out. I usually plan to eat smart most the time, but things happen. Maybe I'll have a cocktail and some bar bites with friends, a meal I order will be prepared with more oil than I'd like, or I'll have a few bites of a dessert that I really love. But since I eat well most of the time, I'm able to indulge every once in a while without worrying too much about it. And if I go too far overboard, I just eat a little lighter the next day and step up the exercise. It's all about figuring out what's best for your lifestyle and being realistic, mindful, and honest about what you're eating.

TRIGGER FOODS

What exactly are trigger foods? Well, they differ from person to person, but one thing remains the same across the board . . . Once you start eating them, it's extremely difficult to stop. They might send you into an eating frenzy or cause you to crave *more* food for the entire day! Everyone has different triggers. For some people (like me), it's salty snacks like crackers and chips—I've gone through an entire multi-serving bag of chips in one sitting. (Yup, this happens to me, too!) For others, it's chocolate and sweets. (Everyone has a friend who can inhale an entire bag of M&Ms or a pint of ice cream . . . or BOTH!) I typically try to avoid my trigger foods, but when I do treat myself to them, I use some tricks . . .

Find single-serving options. Since I love nuts but can't be trusted around big bags of them, I keep 100-calorie packs handy. Mini bags of 94% fat-free microwave popcorn are great for popcorn fans. If your favorite snack doesn't come packaged in single servings, try this next tip.

Break large bags up into mini bags/containers with a single portion in each. This TOTALLY helps. In fact, I recommend doing it as soon as you get back from the store—keep those giant snack bags out of your home whenever possible.

Pop a mint or a piece of sugar-free mint gum right after you have a serving of your trigger food. The mintiness can help stop you from craving more of that food. (The fresh breath is an added bonus.) This one works extremely well.

PORTION-CONTROL TIPS

Look for portion-controlled products.

I have to state the obvious here. Having prepackaged single servings is one of the best ways to avoid overeating. For snacks like cookies and crackers, pick up 100-calorie packs of your favorites. For desserts, go for sugar-free pudding snacks (with 60 calories or less) and individual cups or bars of light ice cream. So seek out portion-controlled foods. It REALLY does help.

Buy in bulk, but portion it all out ASAP.

Single-serve treats can get pricey, so buy multi-serving shelf-stable items, and stock up on sealable plastic baggies and/or containers. Then as soon as you get home from the supermarket, divvy up your goodies into individual servings. It's worth the small amount of extra time it takes.

Use smaller bowls and plates.

Some dishes are ENORMOUS, and they can make realistic portions appear tiny and sad. (Who wants a cereal bowl that's only a third of the way full?) There are even some cute color-coded sets that can be used for both measuring and eating. Very helpful and convenient.

When it comes to foods you eat regularly, familiarize yourself with how their serving sizes look.

This way, when you're out and don't have access to measuring cups or food scales, you'll have a pretty solid idea of what a serving looks like.

TOP INGREDIENT SWAPS

Instead of Sweet Potatoes . . .

Butternut Squash
The taste and texture of butternut squash are very similar to those of sweet potatoes, but the squash is much lower in starchy carbs and calories. It's perfect for fries (like the recipe on page 209), casseroles, soups, and stews! It's even good mashed with a little light butter, salt, and pepper.

Instead of Eggs . . .

Fat-Free Liquid Egg Substitute
This is one of the easiest and most effective swaps you can make. Just replace each egg in a recipe with ¼ cup of the substitute. You'll save around 45 calories and 5 grams of fat for each egg you swap out, and those numbers add up fast! Egg Beaters Original is my go-to egg substitute. It's essentially egg whites with a few added nutrients. Use it in pretty much any recipe that calls for eggs. Egg whites work, too.

Instead of Regular Ground Beef . . .

Extra-Lean Ground Beef, Lean Ground Turkey, or Ground-Beef-Style Soy Crumbles
Extra-lean beef (4 percent fat or less) will save you major calories and fat while maintaining that real beef flavor. Lean turkey (7 percent fat or less) is also an excellent guilt-free alternative, and it tastes much better than extra-lean ground turkey. By the way, regular (not lean) ground turkey can have as many calories and fat grams as regular ground beef, so don't make the mistake of grabbing it at the market. Soy crumbles (like the ones from Boca and MorningStar Farms) will slim down your dish the most, and they have a great beefy taste—just thaw them, season them, and use like cooked ground beef!

TOP INGREDIENT SWAPS

Instead of Pasta . . . .

House Foods Tofu Shirataki Noodle Substitute

It's AMAZING that an entire bag of these noodles has only 20 calories. Use them to make fettuccine Alfredo (page 136) or the lightest lo mein in the universe (page 163). Just rinse, drain, and dry them thoroughly for optimal results. Other pasta swaps to consider? Spaghetti squash (completely AMAZING!), zucchini (cut into ribbons), and broccoli cole slaw (a Hungry Girl staple). Use 'em solo, or mix them with real noodles.

Instead of Sour Cream . . .

Fat-Free Greek Yogurt

To be fair, this stuff is much more than a swap for sour cream. It's perfect for creamy scoopable salads, breakfast bowls, and straight-up snacking. It ALSO happens to pack the creaminess and zing of sour cream with the added bonus of lots of protein, few calories, and no fat. Fat-free Greek yogurt is a total SUPERSTAR.

For more survival strategies, recipes, food finds, and tips 'n tricks, sign up for FREE daily emails at hungry-girl.com!

MAGICAL FOOD EXPANDERS

Portabellas and More Mushrooms!
One large portabella mushroom or 2 cups of chopped mushrooms has roughly 35 calories, 2 grams of fiber, and 3 grams of protein. Mushrooms are especially good at expanding meat dishes, like fajitas, meatloaves, and page 166's beef tacos. The texture and taste work perfectly with beef.

Zucchini!
A medium zucchini has around 30 calories, 2 grams of fiber, and 2.5 grams of protein. So what can it expand? Pasta! Whether it's thinly peeled like fettuccine or cut into slabs similar to lasagna noodles, zucchini does a masterful job of impersonating pasta for hardly any calories at all. Brilliant!

Cauliflower!
A cup of chopped cauliflower has about 30 calories, 2 grams of fiber, and 2 grams of protein. And its expanding ability is the stuff of legend. Cauliflower is a go-to super-sizer when it comes to starchy dishes—anything with potatoes, pasta, or rice. It blends in seamlessly . . .

Broccoli Cole Slaw!
This mix of shredded broccoli stems with other veggies clocks in at 25 calories, 3 grams of fiber, and 2 grams of protein per cup. Plus, it couldn't be more convenient. Pre-shredded, pre-washed . . . Some can even be steamed in the bag. Use it to expand spaghetti dishes, stir-frys, and even meatloaf!

MAGICAL FOOD EXPANDERS

94% Fat-Free Microwave Popcorn!
You can eat about 5 cups of this popcorn for 100 calories and 1.5 grams of fat, plus 4 grams of fiber. For a large-and-in-charge snack mix, combine popcorn with measured amounts of delicious (yet somewhat calorie-dense) goodies like nuts, mini chocolate chips, and cereal.

Frozen-Meal Filler-Uppers!
Light entrées from the freezer aisle can be great when you're in a hurry, but the portion sizes can be pretty small. Adding vegetables is an easy way to make 'em more substantial. And since those dinners typically come with a LOT of sauce, you can easily stir in some microwaved frozen veggies. For pasta-based meals, I like to add steamed broccoli cole slaw or bean sprouts (not alfalfa sprouts—bean sprouts are more substantial and taste better here). These have a similar texture to noodles, and the bean sprouts work perfectly in Asian-style dinners!

BETTER-FOR-YOU CRAVING-BUSTERS

Pizza

I like to keep single-serving, heat-and-eat, better-for-you pizza options on hand. There are many solid options in the freezer aisle. Seek out ones that have 300 calories or less and no more than 10 grams of fat—a few grams of fiber is a plus!

> **D.I.Y. . . .**
> Pizza-fied Chicken with Saucy Spaghetti Swap (page 170)
> Perfect Pizza-bella (page 211)

Ice Cream

Light ice cream is an obvious (and delicious!) choice. But I tend to go for portion-controlled picks, since ice cream is one of the most commonly over-served foods. (Take a second to envision half a cup of it. It's probably WAY smaller than the amount of ice cream you typically scoop into your dessert bowl!) Go for light ice cream bars, low-fat ice cream sandwiches, low-fat fudge pops, or individual cups of light ice cream. Keep the calorie counts at 150 or less per serving.

French Fries

Your best weapons here are a big knife, an oven, and the right vegetables. Butternut squash and carrots make much lighter fries than conventional fried spuds. Just cut, bake, and eat. You can enjoy these alone as a fry swap, or bake and mix them with real potatoes that have been cut into fry shapes. It's all good!

> **D.I.Y. . . .**
> Snack-tastic Butternut Fries (page 209)
> Easy Baked Carrot Fries (page 210)

BETTER-FOR-YOU CRAVING-BUSTERS

Chocolatey Desserts
For chocolate-cake cravings, find options that have 100 calories or less and lots of fiber. Vitalicious treats—VitaTops, Mini VitaCakes, VitaBrownies, etc.—fit the bill and are some of my favorites! There are also MANY options for frozen low-fat fudge bars. And if you just want something warm and chocolatey to sip, grab a packet of hot cocoa mix with 30 calories or less.

> **D.I.Y. . . .**
> Chocolate-Chip-Stuffed Strawberries (page 217)
> Cannoli Bites (page 219)

Potato Chips
I love baked chips (regular and tortilla) as well as popped chips! Look for 100-calorie bags to keep portions in check. I'm also a fan of 94% fat-free microwave popcorn (look for mini bags) when cravings for crunchy snacks hit.

> **D.I.Y. . . .**
> Baked Kale Chips (page 200)
> D.I.Y. Tortilla Chips (page 212)

Pies and Pastries
I like to create guilt-free baked goodies using store-bought reduced-fat dough and mini fillo shells. Not looking to cook? Try dessert-flavored light yogurt, and snack bars in decadent, pastry-like flavors.

> **D.I.Y. . . .**
> Upside-Down Cream Pie (page 201)
> Apple Pie in a Mug (page 203)
> Upside-Down Strawberry Pie (page 213)

FOOD FAKERS

These are foods that SOUND like they should be smart options but they're not. Don't be fooled . . .

Restaurant Salads

Despite what you may have thought for most of your life, salads are NOT always a safe choice when dining out. Full-fat dressing, cheese, fried toppings, and more can all contribute to sky-high calorie counts. Even the most innocent-sounding salads can be full-on nutritional nightmares. Read menus carefully, and pay attention to what comes on that salad. Don't be afraid to make special requests when it comes to leaving things off your greens. As for dressing, find a light option and get it on the side. Then dip, don't pour . . .

Flavored Water

Many products call themselves "water," even when they're fully flavored and sweetened. Some of these are reasonable options and some of them are not. Many popular "water" beverages have 50 calories per 8-ounce serving . . . but the standard 20-ounce bottles have 125 calories each, not to mention more than 30 grams of sugar! Read those labels . . .

Turkey, Fish, and Veggie Burgers

In general, yes—turkey, fish, and veggie options are often lighter than fatty beef dishes served at restaurants. But they're not always as guilt-free as they sound. Do your research first, and see if you can find the nutritional info beforehand. No time? Make special requests—ask for the burger wrapped in lettuce leaves instead of a bun, skip the cheese, and top it with tomatoes and onions!

FOOD FAKERS

Veggie Chips/Crisps

Just because a crunchy snack has "veggie" in its name, that doesn't necessarily mean it's good for you. Sometimes these things are simply veggie flavored and contain a scant amount of real vegetables. Plus, they're typically fattening due to an abundance of that three-letter chip foe—OIL. Even the healthiest food in the world will become fatty and high in calories if it's fried in too much oil.

Smoothies

"Smoothie" is one of those terms with a health halo over it, meaning it sounds more nutritious than it actually is. Not all smoothies are smart choices. Many of them have WAY too much added sugar (sometimes in the form of straight-up syrup) and other high-calorie add-ins. Plus, they're often too large and tossed back like basic beverages when they're more like meal replacements or substantial snacks. (Flip to page 205 for a 100-calorie smoothie!)

Granola

Oats and grains are great for you . . . just not when they're coated with lots of sugar and cooked in too much oil or butter. And while granola is okay in small portions, many people eat it like cereal, so the calories add up FAST. Even low-fat granola typically has close to 400 calories per cup! This is yet another case in which you NEED to check the labels. Don't just check the calories and fat content, though. Take a look at the serving size, because it's typically VERY small . . .

FOOD FAKERS

Dried Fruit

While fruit is great for you, tiny servings with too many calories are not. A third of a cup of raisins isn't much, yet it contains more calories than THREE CUPS of fresh strawberries. Plus, dried fruit is sometimes sweetened with sugar. One of the worst offenders is banana chips; not only are they sugary, but they're also usually FRIED. Crave dehydrated fruit? Go for freeze-dried. Store shelves are packed with great options that have big portion sizes, small calorie counts, and no added sugar. Plus, crunchy foods are more fun to eat.

Not-So-Single Servings

Just because something LOOKS like one serving doesn't mean it is "one serving" (as defined by the nutritional panel). Deceptive packaging doesn't always mean those foods are off-limits, but be smart: Check the Servings Per Container portion of the nutrition panel, and do a little math if need be. Canned soup is a great example, since most people consume the entire two-serving can. A can of low-fat soup can still be a good choice, but remember to multiply the stats.

EMERGENCY SNACKS

These are guilt-free foods that can be stored in a backpack, purse, mini fridge, or desk drawer. They're your best defense against bad decisions when hunger unexpectedly hits. Here's a rundown of the best emergency snacks to have around . . .

Filling Snack Bars with Protein and Fiber

These aren't just for cases of idle munchies. These are meant to annihilate your hunger. And since there are SO many bars out there, I'm naming names here. Fruit 'n nut bars (like the ones from Kind) hold up well on the go and taste great. Crunchy granola bars (like the twofers sold by Nature Valley) are another smart choice. But my number-one brand of stashable snack bars? Quest Bars. The texture is perfect, the flavors are AMAZING, and the protein and fiber counts are through the roof. In general, I stick with bars that have 200 calories or less.

Salty Crunchy Snacks

Sure, you can get crunch from vegetables—but sometimes chips are the only answer. Since they're a trigger food for me, when I DO indulge in salty, crunchy snack foods, I stick with 100-calorie bags of lightened-up versions. Another favorite of mine? Seaweed snacks! If you haven't tried these yet, I suggest you do. Even if you think you don't like seaweed, you might fall in love with these seasoned-up crispy snacks. Yum!

Fresh Fruit

Fuji apples are a consistent favorite of mine, bananas and oranges are excellent grab-n-go picks (since they come in their own cases!), and tossing a bunch of grapes into a baggie or sealable container is always a nice, simple snack. You'll almost never find me without a giant apple nearby . . . I eat one pretty much every day!

EMERGENCY SNACKS

Ready-to-Eat Veggies
It's easy to say, "Cut up vegetables! Snack on them!" But then comes the response, "I like veggies but don't have time to chop them every morning." Instead of just NOT eating veggies, find choices that require less prep—cherry tomatoes, snap peas, baby carrots, or even pre-cut broccoli florets. Another staple emergency snack!

100-Calorie Packs of Nuts
A bag of portion-controlled nuts is a wonderful snack—filling, loaded with nutrients, *and* easy to stash. Plus, it's pretty hard to crush one to smithereens, no matter how full your purse/backpack/briefcase is. If you want to save cash, buy a giant bag of nuts, and *immediately* divvy it up. You can have around ½ ounce of almonds or pistachios (about 12 almonds or 24 pistachios) for a hundred calories.

Some Refrigeration Required . . .
Light dairy snacks deserve their own shelf in the fridge. Mini Babybel, the beloved line of wax-coated cheese wheels, is a personal favorite. Light string cheese is another staple of mine. And both of those will be fine in your purse for short excursions. When it comes to yogurt, I'm never without fat-free Greek yogurt and traditional fat-free yogurt. Those 6-ounce containers are perfect for snacking.

For more survival strategies, recipes, food finds, and tips 'n tricks, sign up for FREE daily emails at hungry-girl.com!

DINING-OUT
SURVIVAL GUIDES

The Dining Out on the Plan section (page 98) provides quick
tips and specific options that fit perfectly into the four-week
jump-start plan. You can (and should!) incorporate these meals
into your continued weight loss or maintenance. And for some
anytime picks, skips, and tips 'n tricks (a.k.a. survival strategies!),
this portion of the book has everything you need . . .

DOs & DON'Ts for Dining Out . . .

DON'T starve yourself before a big meal out. It might seem like a good idea to "save your calories" for dinner, but it's not. You'll arrive starving and be more likely to pounce on the bread basket, order a heavy appetizer, and make other bad decisions when choosing your main meal. Eat normally during the day. Then have a glass of water before you leave for the restaurant, and another one when you arrive.

DO your research. Google is your friend. Even without the nutritional info, it's helpful to know what's available in advance. This way, you can take your time reviewing everything on the menu and deciding which is your best bet. You can also do a little investigating. Wondering about the chicken marsala at your local Italian restaurant? Look up similar dishes on other websites that provide stats.

DON'T be afraid to special order. Most restaurants are happy to accommodate requests, as long as you're polite about it. If you want to know how something is prepared, just ask. If the baked chicken on the menu comes bathed in cream sauce, request it on the side. The worst they can do is say no.

DO take it easy with the cocktails. Not only do those calories add up quickly, but once you've had a couple of drinks, it's harder to turn down a decadent dessert. For more on bar survival strategies, flip to page 260.

GO-ANYWHERE MENU ADVICE

Bread

Avoid making eye contact with whatever free starchy foods come to the table. I once heard a staggering statistic about how many calories' worth of bread and butter people typically indulge in before dinner . . . FIVE HUNDRED! Sometimes, if my dinner mates are on board, I'll ask the waiter to hold the bread.

Appetizers

I fully support appetizers. I typically start off a meal with a broth-based soup or shrimp cocktail. I especially like soup because studies show that starting a meal with broth-based soup could actually cause you to take in about 20 percent fewer calories overall during that meal.

Salads

Whether it's a starter or your main meal, always order the dressing on the side—light, if available. Then dip, don't pour. Dressing is another major calorie contributor when dining out, so sticking with the light stuff and using it sparingly can instantly save you hundreds of calories.

You may want to order ingredients like cheese and nuts on the side, too. These are generally high in fat, and getting them on the side makes it easy to evaluate exactly how much you're getting. Then you can control the amount you add.

GO-ANYWHERE MENU ADVICE

Entreés

When I'm handed a menu, I immediately scan it for the best options. Look for words like "grilled," "steamed," "broiled," and "baked." I skip over entrées that are fried and avoid red flags like "cheesy," "creamy," and "buttery." I recommend sticking with entrées that center around lean protein and are served with vegetables. Some of my favorites are grilled chicken, broiled fish, and lean steak—a filet is the leanest cut, and you can usually order a petite. I generally order sauces on the side, and I stick with tomato-based options. And I LOVE baked potatoes. Go for a small one (or take half home for another day). Have it plain or with some marinara sauce or salsa in place of butter or sour cream.

Desserts

If you're going to order dessert, SPLIT it! Restaurant desserts often have a meal's worth of calories apiece. So if you want something decadent, pair a few bites with coffee. Better yet . . . order fresh fruit. Even if it isn't on the menu as an option, many places have it on hand.

Italian Food

PICKS: Minestrone soup, steamed mussels or clams, and a small salad (oil & vinegar or light dressing on the side). For the main course, grilled fish or chicken and a side of vegetables. Season with lemon juice or balsamic vinegar, or top with marinara sauce. If you need pasta, make it a side order, and ask about whole-wheat alternatives (the fiber makes them more filling). Coffee and biscotti are the perfect meal ending.

SKIPS: Fried appetizers (calamari, mozzarella, etc.), garlic bread, and oily pasta salads are bad starters. Alfredo is a no-no, and anything with "Parmesan" in the name will likely be fried and covered in cheese. And remember: Heavy dressings can sink a simple salad.

Mexican Food

PICKS: Ceviche is a great light appetizer pick. And here's how to tailor a fajita plate: Ask if the meat, chicken, or shrimp can be cooked with little to no oil. Use just a couple of tortillas, and pack them full of veggies and salsa. Skip sour cream, rice, and cheese. Black beans are great as long as they're not smothered in cheese. P.S. When I eat spicy food, I tend to fill up a little faster, so I love extra jalapeños.

SKIPS: Nix the tortilla chips (especially those in bottomless baskets!) and huge frozen margaritas. When it comes to chimichangas, chalupas, enchiladas, tostadas, empanadas (all the other *adas*!) . . . You're dealing with lots of oily, cheesy and in some cases FRIED items. And tortilla salad bowls are a huge DON'T—the crispy shell typically has WAY more fat and calories than the actual salad.

Chinese Food

PICKS: Start with soup (egg drop, hot & sour, or wonton), and order a steamed protein + vegetable dish with the sauce on the side. If you need rice, stick with brown and keep the serving size small (half a cup). And use those chopsticks! You'll eat more slowly (unless you're a total pro), so you're less likely to overdo it before your brain gets the message you're full. And with just around 35 calories each, fortune cookies are a big yes.

SKIPS: Anything fried (from chicken to rice to those crispy wontons), heavy noodle dishes, and too much sauce.

Japanese Food/Sushi

PICKS: Miso soup, edamame, sunomono (cucumber and vinegar) salad, seaweed salad, and sashimi. When ordering sushi, ask for it to be made with less rice than usual. And see if brown rice is an option—bonus fiber! Wasabi and ginger are great, and soy sauce is low in calories—just go easy if you're watching your salt. If you're not a sushi fan, go for chicken teriyaki, but make sure it's white meat and not dark. And go easy on that sweet sauce!

SKIPS: Anything with the words "tempura," "dynamite," or "crunch." Those are buzzwords for fried items and mayo-based sauces. Avoid rolls made with mayo mixed into the filling . . . and anything made with cream cheese!

Buffets and Salad Bars

BEFORE you hit the buffet, drink a glass of water.
It'll take the edge off your hunger. Then take a full lap around and look at EVERYTHING. Take small amounts of the splurges you really want to indulge in, and fill your plate with the lighter items. Only go back for seconds if you're truly still hungry. Have a glass of water first, and wait five minutes to see how you feel.

PICKS: Shrimp cocktail (jackpot!), fresh fruit, cut veggies with salsa, broth-based soups, leafy salad greens, lean deli meats, grilled or baked chicken or fish, steamed or grilled veggies, egg-white omelettes (if it's a breakfast buffet) . . . Lots of good options! If there's a salad bar, top your greens with fresh veggies (tomatoes, mushrooms, cucumbers, bell peppers, etc.), salsa, lean protein (like flaked tuna, turkey, chicken), and beans (black, garbanzo, kidney, etc.).

SKIPS: Cheesy casseroles, fried chicken or fish, creamy pasta, pizza, creamy soups, deep-fried foods, and (in the case of breakfast) sweet carby items like waffles and French toast. At the salad bar, avoid croutons, tortilla strips, fried noodles, full-fat cheeses and dressings, and any scoopable salads soaked in oil or coated in mayo.

Coffee Shops

Do your homework. Most coffee chains have websites with detailed nutritional information. Go online to see what's what—find something you like that doesn't have a huge number of calories and fat, and order THAT. Try not to walk in without doing a little research.

Sweeten it yourself. Whenever possible, order your drinks unsweetened, and then add your favorite no-calorie sweetener. Whether it's the blue packets (aspartame), the pink packets (saccharine), the yellow packets (sucralose), or the green packets (stevia), pick your no-calorie sweetener of choice. I always keep some of my favorite packets in my purse.

Ditch the fat. Switching from regular or reduced-fat milk to skim/fat-free milk can save you dozens of calories and a lot of fat. Just do it!

Avoid outrageously large sizes. There's no reason to order drinks the size of popcorn buckets. Stick with something petite.

As tempting as they are, skip the cakes, cookies, muffins, and scones. Even reduced-fat ones have hundreds of calories. Not worth it. Fruit and light yogurt, though, are definite yeses. Just watch out for granola toppings—those can add a few hundred calories and a lot of fat!

Want to add flavor to your hot and cold drinks without adding calories? Ask for a pump (or two) of sugar-free syrup. Typically they'll have at least vanilla and hazelnut, but some coffee chains have even more fun flavors.

Ask about flavored coffees. See if they're made from flavored coffee beans (which are virtually calorie-free), or if the flavoring is added later with sugary syrups or powders. That'll make a difference in the calorie counts.

Skip the whip. Whipped cream is delicious, but it can easily add about a HUNDRED fatty calories to your order. Not worth it. Instead, ask for some nonfat foamed milk on top . . .

Fast Food

Most chains put all their nutritional information online. Don't be lazy! Check out the menus and stats before you go out—or whenever you have some free time. You can really learn a lot.

Chicken is *typically* a better choice than a burger—but make sure you order it GRILLED, not fried or crispy. You can usually get grilled chicken on salads *and* sandwiches.

Instead of getting special sauce or mayo, stick with mustard and/or ketchup. That'll save you a lot of calories and fat grams.

Order your sandwiches or burgers on "lettuce buns," a.k.a. wrapped in lettuce. Skipping the bread is a great way to save about 200 calories. If the person taking your order balks at the term "lettuce bun," just ask for your sandwich goodies over extra lettuce.

Don't drink your calories. Pass on sugary lemonade, regular soda, and shakes. Stick with water, unsweetened iced tea, or diet soda.

Smaller and simpler = lighter options. Don't get sucked in by the limited-time-only special mega burger. "But I have to get it now or it'll be gone!" Good, fine, let it be gone.

Fast Food

Food Fakers: Fast-Food Edition

Fast-food salads can be ridiculously fattening. Common culprits include fried chicken, tortilla shells, noodles, nuts, too much cheese, and fatty dressings. So order smart. Choose the lightest dressing, and only use half a packet. And those crunchy salad toppers often come on the side, so just ask that they be left out. And never ever order anything that comes in a giant taco shell!

Fish sandwiches are NOT always good options. They're pretty much always fried and served with creamy tartar sauce. They often have MORE calories than burgers. So skip the fatty fish . . .

Don't let words like FRESH and PREMIUM fool you. They are often deceptive. Look up the nutritional facts, or pay very close attention to the ingredients. If cheese and mayo are involved, chances are the calorie count is going to be pretty high.

Ice Cream & Frozen Yogurt Shops

Serving sizes can be deceiving. The serving size listed with the stats is usually much smaller than what ends up in your cup. While ½ cup is a typical amount listed with calorie counts, when was the last time you had 8 measly tablespoons of fro yo? Just think about that towering swirl extending out of the cup! If you're looking at nutritional info, get ready to do some multiplication.

Look for fat-free and light options. Stick with small portions and avoid sundaes and shakes. When it comes to toppings, heap on the fresh fruit, and finish it off with a low-calorie topper like a few crushed cone pieces, some sprinkles (only about 20 calories per teaspoon), or a bit of sweet cereal.

Skip the big cones, but indulge in a small cake cone or sugar cone. The little cones are fantastic because they can only hold so much! Plus, the calorie counts are nice and low. Cake cones, the flat-bottomed ones, generally have 20 to 25 calories, and standard sugar cones have 45 to 60 calories each.

Other Snacking Locations...

Movie theaters—Oversized theater snacks are some of the worst, so bring your own! Lollipops and pre-popped mini bags of 94% fat-free popcorn are great. If you're at the mercy of the concession stand, go for fat-free hard candy or gummis, and stick to one serving. (Check the servings per container!) And sip water or diet soda. If you HAVE to have popcorn, make it a small one, and do NOT let them put any butter on it.

Mall food courts—Check out all your options before ordering. Delis and Mexican places are great for salads topped with lean protein. Pack emergency snacks, and plan accordingly. And never hit the mall hungry!

For more survival strategies, recipes, food finds, and tips 'n tricks, sign up for FREE daily emails at hungry-girl.com!

Party Time!

Special occasions are a time for celebration, but they don't have to be a time for consuming too many calories. Here's how I party . . . guilt-free!

Top Party Tips

1. Don't go to a party on an empty stomach. Eat a little snack before heading out. This way, you won't arrive hungry and inhale the first thing you see.

2. Make something guilt-free and delicious, and take it to the party with you. You'll have something smart to snack on, and your host will likely be thankful for the help.

3. Don't start eating right away. Socialize first. That'll take the focus off the food, and give you time to decide if you're really even hungry. Don't just grab the first thing you see . . .

4. Look for simple foods that have a lot of protein and fiber. You'll be less likely to overeat those because they're filling, and even if you do, it's the good stuff. Shrimp cocktail, crudités, and lean grilled meats are all great party staples.

5. Avoid anything cheesy, fried, or shiny, like side dishes with lots of mayo, oily appetizers, fatty dips, or deep-fried ANYTHING. Macaroni salad, artichoke dip, and popcorn shrimp—those are all high in fat and calories.

Party Time!

TOP ATE Tips for Big Holiday Meals

Holiday meals can contain around 3,000 calories and over 200 fat grams. That is obviously too many calories to have at once. Here's how to make sure you don't overdo it . . .

1. Eat breakfast and a high-protein lunch before the big meal. If you restrict yourself during the day, you'll eat way too much at dinner, and you'll probably go for the really fattening stuff.

2. Get some exercise. The more calories you burn with activity, the more you can indulge a little at dinner. If you can't get in a full workout, take a nice long walk after the big meal.

3. Drink a lot of water throughout the day and before your meal. It'll keep you hydrated and feeling full.

4. Start with a salad and/or soup. Green salads and broth-based soups are filling and typically very low in calories and fat. They'll help take the edge off your hunger, so by the time you dive into the entrées and sides, you won't need huge portions to feel satisfied. If you have a salad, remember to stick with light dressing. (Dip, don't pour.)

5. Fill your plate mostly with lean meat and healthy side dishes. Then add small amounts of the decadent side dishes.

6. If you're eating turkey, stick with white meat and don't eat the skin. It'll give you the most bang for your calorie buck. Dark meat has about 15 percent more calories and 30 to 40 percent more fat than white meat.

Party Time!

TOP ATE Tips for Big Holiday Meals (continued)

7. Don't deprive yourself of your favorite things. Treat yourself! Just be smart about it and take small portions. If you've been thinking about Grandma's apple pie all year and then try to avoid it altogether, you may end up raiding the fridge when everyone's asleep.

8. Resist the urge to wear your baggiest pants. I'm not saying you should wear TIGHT PANTS, but if you wear clothes that are a little formfitting, you'll be less likely to overeat. Trust me on this one . . .

Most importantly, if you splurge, just get right back on track the next day. It's called a *splurge* for a reason—it's not supposed to be an everyday occurrence. And if you're not careful, it's easy to let one night of heavy eating turn into several. So discipline yourself to get back on the smart-eating wagon—then you'll feel more comfortable the next time you want to enjoy an indulgent meal. And if you're the host, send guests home with leftovers, so you're not tempted to eat decadent food for days!

Party Time!

How Fancy Is This Party?

It's Pretty Fancy!

PICKS: Chilled seafood (shrimp, crabmeat, clams, etc.), grilled chicken or beef skewers, fresh vegetables (but skip creamy dips and dressings), mini bruschetta.

SKIPS: Pigs in a blanket, mini quiches, anything fried, cheesy flatbreads or pizzas, stuffed mushrooms.

HOT TIP! Instead of grabbing something every time a tray passes, fill a small plate once and use a fork. It's easier to control yourself when you can see how much you're eating. And keep your hands full—hold a drink, or your purse . . . or both. You'll be less likely to reach for food if a balancing act is required!

It's Pretty Casual . . .

PICKS: Turkey slices from a deli tray, veggies with salsa, baked chips (watch your portions), fruit or fruit salad.

SKIPS: Nachos, layered dips, fried chicken, greasy chips, anything cheesy or fried, bowls of nuts.

HOT TIP! Don't sit or stand too close to the food table. If it's right in front of your face, and you can see or smell it, you'll be more likely to eat it.

Bars

A shot of most hard liquors (vodka, rum, tequila, etc.) has around 100 calories. My go-to cocktail? A shot of flavored vodka with club soda and a splash of fruit juice—blueberry vodka with soda water and a splash of pineapple juice is a great combo! And as you might suspect, clear alcohols have fewer calories than creamy liqueurs. One tiny shot of Baileys Irish Cream has around 150 calories and 7 grams of fat!

Tonic-water warning! Club soda has no calories, while tonic water has about 80 calories per cup. Beware!

Wine is a good option. A 5-ounce glass of wine has about 120 calories. And studies show that red wine can be good for your heart. And if you're craving a beer, choose something light, preferably in a bottle—you'll get 12 ounces rather than the 16 ounces in a pint glass.

Three Things to Remember . . .

1. Take it slow. Alternating alcoholic beverages with water (or a no-calorie nonalcoholic drink) is a great way to pace yourself and keep your calorie intake down. Try not to drink more than one alcoholic beverage per hour.

2. It's not all about the drinks. Take a lap around the bar—talk with your friends, play a game of darts, shoot some pool, or step outside for some fresh air.

3. Bar food is NOT your friend. Nachos, Buffalo wings, and giant bowls of mixed nuts—PASS. In a pinch, steal the celery and carrot sticks from that plate of Buffalo wings and dip 'em in salsa.

At the Office . . .

You spend SO much time at work and are likely faced with a LOT of temptation there. Here are some general guidelines . . .

Morning Prep
Eat breakfast before you get to work. Once you arrive, you might find donuts, muffins, and bagels with cream cheese waiting for you in the kitchen or break room. If you've skipped breakfast, that food is going to be *way* harder to pass up. Not hungry first thing in the morning? Have a piece of fruit, and bring a smart morning meal with you. If you have a fridge in your office, keep fat-free Greek yogurt and (if you have a microwave) Egg Beaters on hand. You can make yourself a Fruit 'n Yogurt Bowl or an Egg Mug.

Break-Room Brilliance
So how do you avoid the temptation of sweets and snacks in the break room? If you show up at work without emergency snacks, you could be in trouble. So make sure you *always* have smart options. Check out my Must-Have Office Snacks on the next page!

Lunch Lessons
If you're having a catered-lunch meeting, stick with lean deli meats, lettuce, and tomato—you can usually put together a little deli salad. If the team is ordering in, ask to see the menu, and special order if you need to. There's nothing wrong with that. If you're not having a lunch meeting, bring your own food, or order in. I think you're better off bringing lunch from home whenever possible. You can save money that way, and you'll know EXACTLY what's in your food.

Birthday-Cake Survival
If you work in an office, there's a good chance that at least once a month you'll be called into a conference room for someone's birthday and see a gigantic frosted cake. No one says you have to eat a full slice of it—or ANY of it for that matter. Either skip it, or take a small slice and eat a bite or two. Another option? Head back to your office, and grab one of your sweet-treat emergency snacks. I like VitaTops during these little cake emergencies.

At the Office . . .

Vending-Machine Mania

I don't think there are any hard-and-fast rules when it comes to vending machines. But there are a lot of food fakers in there—things like multi-serving bags of trail mix and oversized packs of calorie-dense dried fruit. Look for sensible picks like snack bars with protein, fiber, and reasonable calorie counts. It's worth taking a couple of minutes to look up the nutritional information from the snack brand's website. Baked chips are another excellent option.

Calorie-Burning Tips 'n Tricks

If you sit all day at the office, you're not going to burn many calories at all. So take the stairs instead of the elevator, visit people in their offices instead of calling them, hand-deliver documents, use the restroom on a different floor . . .
BE CREATIVE! Small changes can really make a difference.

Must-Have Office Snacks (No Refrigeration Required)

* Canned Soup (Low-Sodium or Reduced-Sodium)
* 100-Calorie Bags of Baked or Popped Chips
* Snack Bars with Protein and Fiber
* Tuna Pouches
* 94% Fat-Free Microwave Popcorn Mini Bags
* Apples, Oranges, Pears, and Bananas
* 100-Calorie Packs of Almonds

If You Have a Fridge/Freezer . . .

* Fat-Free Yogurt (Greek or Regular)
* Cut Veggies with Salsa or Low-Fat Dip
* Lean Turkey Slices (Low-Sodium or Reduced-Sodium)
* Light String Cheese
* Fruit Salad
* Low-Fat Frozen Fudge Pops and Fruit Bars

Travel Survival Guide

Whether you're on a business trip or a vacation, sticking to an eating plan isn't easy when you're traveling. But with the right tips 'n tricks in your back pocket, it's completely possible to eat smart on the go.

Before You Fly . . .

If you're traveling by plane, there's a good chance you're going to have a long stretch of time where your eating situation may feel a little out of your control. The key is to remain IN control, and it's easier than you might think.

Pack emergency snacks! Keep a mini stash of foods that are high in protein and/or fiber, don't require a lot of room, and won't get squished in your carry-on bag. These will keep you going between meals and prevent you from tearing through one of those gargantuan snack boxes. Mess-free fruit (like Fuji apples), snack bars with protein and fiber, and 100-calorie packs of almonds are all excellent travel companions.

Don't board hungry. Snacks are well and good, but don't forget about meals. And while some airlines are getting better about providing calorie-conscious food options, others are not. Leave yourself time to shop around in the terminal for the best fit—many airports have salads and other meal options that are better than picks offered on the plane.

Keep hydrated. Air travel can dry you out and make you thirsty (which can also make you feel hungrier), and the drink cart doesn't come by that often. So snag a big bottle of water from an airport shop before boarding.

Travel Survival Guide

Up In the Air . . .

It's okay to say yes to one of those little bags of peanuts or pretzels. Either one is actually a great little snack, because the portion size is perfect. The peanuts are best because they have healthy fats and a little protein boost. I also love drinking tomato juice on airplanes for some reason—it really helps keep me from feeling hungry, and it's very low in calories.

When they say it's okay to walk around the cabin, go for it. Stretch your legs and keep your blood flowing. It'll keep you alert and feeling good!

Travel Survival Guide

Once You Arrive . . .

Do your research. If your hotel doesn't have any decent breakfast options, see what's available at the place next door. Find out if your room has a mini fridge or if one's available—then you can stock it with smart snacks, like fat-free or low-fat yogurt, cut veggies, and light string cheese. If you're on a cruise, ask in advance if special requests can be accommodated. You get the picture!

Make daily activity a part of your trip. One way to counteract extra calorie intake? Get in some extra exercise! Go for a morning walk or jog each day, and take advantage of any fun vacation activities like swimming, hiking, and exploring. And walk as much as possible. Don't cut corners and take cabs if places are within walking distance. Urban trekking is fun, and it's great exercise.

Avoid that hotel minibar. It can be tempting having all those items in your room, 24 hours a day. There are three simple ways to resist it. One, if they give you a key to unlock the minibar when you check in, say "No thanks." Two, bring your own stash of goodies. Three, look at the price list—any desire you had to tear into a container of candied nuts will fly out the window when you see that it costs $13.50. Not worth it in SO many ways.

Don't sweat the small stuff. Staying on top of calorie counts while you're out of town is tough, so try not to stress out too much. You're on vacation, after all, so enjoy it! If you want to share that tiramisu with your family at lunch or have a tropical cocktail with dinner, do it! Just make really good choices for the rest of the day. And if you overdo it for a day or two, don't let it ruin your trip. Just get some extra exercise in the next day, and make smarter food choices as well. And when you return, jump right back into your routine.

THERE YOU HAVE IT!

Every Hungry Girl weight-loss and weight-maintenance strategy you'll need to help you succeed—all in one place! I hope you LOVE this book as much as I do. Have questions, comments, or just want to say hi? Email me at ask@hungry-girl.com. And for all the latest guilt-free recipes, food finds, and tips 'n tricks, visit hungry-girl.com and sign up for free daily emails!

'Til next time . . . Chew the right thing!

Lisa :)

INDEX